the powells.com interviews

◆

the powells.com interviews

◆

22 Authors and Artists Talk About Their Books

Dave Weich

iUniverse.com, Inc.
San Jose New York Lincoln Shanghai

The Powells.com Interviews
22 Authors and Artists Talk About Their Books

Published by iUniverse.com, Inc.

For information address:
iUniverse.com, Inc.
620 North 48th Street, Suite 201
Lincoln, NE 68504-3467
www.iuniverse.com

Grateful acknowledgement is made to the publishers of the works
discussed in this book for permission to reprint various lines
from the original texts. Owing to limitations of space,
acknowledgements are listed in full in the back pages of this book.

ISBN: 0-595-13245-6

Printed in the United States of America

Don't you think most writers are secretly worried that they're not really writers? That it's all been happenstance, something came together randomly, the letters came together, and they won't coalesce ever again?

Nicholson Baker

Contents

◆

Learn More

Introduction

◆

PowellsBooks.news

<><><><><><><<>>
includes:
what how why
scribbles
where when
the literacy volunteers
acknowledgements
about the interviewer
iUniverse
let it rain
fup. store cat.
<><><><><><<>>

Welcome to the City of Books. The words are about to begin.

What How Why

A project to raise funds for the Literacy Volunteers of America (LVA).

By talking to acclaimed authors and artists about writing and reading, gathering those conversations in a book, and passing our royalties to LVA, an organization that helps people who might not otherwise have the chance to read and write, themselves.

Because as employees of an independent bookstore we spend the bulk of our lives surrounded by books—glossy new paperbacks and eccentric old hardcovers, shelves and shelves, rooms and rooms, floors and floors full of books. And we're constantly thankful for it. It's not that we can't imagine a life without the written word. We'd just like to work toward a world where no one has to live one.

Jin Reconstructs Decades of Chinese Culture Using Common Collection of Scribbles!

A few words about words, then. You'll find many of our favorites in this book. They're the brick and the mortar here, both, the body and the soul. Those who know where to look, who know *how* to look, will find music and pictures in the pages that follow, but all of it's coded in letters.

Many of the words in this volume appear dozens and dozens of times. (Such endurance!) Others, including *wicked* and *purposive*, excel in memorable walk-on roles.

How does Roddy Doyle get us racing through those fetid Dublin sewage tunnels? Did A.M. Homes really write a story about a boy's tempestuous affair with a Barbie doll, or was that a dream? Reading Ian Frazier's *On the Rez*, why do you have the irrepressible urge to tell everyone you see about SuAnne Big Crow?

"Words are charms," Frazier explains.

In *Anil's Ghost*, Booker Prize-winning novelist and poet Michael Ondaatje performs an entire scene *with only six words.*

Ha Jin says, "I think the ultimate goal for a piece of literature is to transcend time to some degree, not to vacate it but to go through it." His novel, *Waiting*, won both the 1999 National Book Award and the 2000 PEN/Faulkner Award for Fiction. Putting words together in a consistently engaging manner over the course of a couple hundred pages, Jin brings readers to China—he *immerses* you in Chinese life.

Words fill the dark and words fill the light. Words are dangerous and words can heal. Words are power.

Where When

Whenever possible, these interviews were conducted in soundproof, underground shelters buried inconspicuously throughout the greater Portland, Oregon area—the better to keep our conversations secret until publication.

Cookies are served. We've found that most authors like cookies. Moreover, preliminary studies suggest that Miel's famous peanut butter chip squares invoke nostalgic lapses in four out of five published authors, thereby instigating colorful (if sometimes unsettling) memories—or, just the kind of personal revelation people associate with the award-winning *Powells.com Interviews* series.

There, the secret's out. So we might as well tell you the whole truth— that we schedule these interviews according to each author's snacking patterns. That's where our in-house staff of spies and dieticians really pays off.

Powells.com is a professional organization; there are no two ways about it.

"Education of the people insures the preservation of their liberties."
   —inscription above the north doors to Grover Cleveland High School, corner of SE 26th Avenue and SE Franklin Street, Portland

The Literacy Volunteers

Thank you.

Literacy Volunteers of America is a national network of more than three hundred fifty locally based programs, supported by state and national staff.

Its mission is to change lives through literacy. Professionally trained volunteer tutors teach *Basic Literacy* and *English for Speakers of Other Languages* to courageous, motivated adults.

Literacy skills enable LVA students to be better parents, workers, and citizens. Their individual gains benefit their families, employers, and society. Learn more about Literacy Volunteers of America in the back pages of this book, then visit their web site at www.literacyvolunteers.org.

Acknowledgements

Some of our favorite words could not be present during the production of this book. Not to diminish their value, every last one, but you can only fit so many words in one collection anyway. *Rhinocerotic*, for instance—one of our favorite words, but rhinoceroses never came up in conversation, nor did their snouty, three-toed characteristics. So it goes.

Among the kind, talented people who helped create this collection are Darin Sennett (especially kind, especially talented), Chris Valaas, Kanth Gopalpur, Chris Farley, Miel Alegre, Nathan Ruckman, Malia Susee, Amy Antonio, Ann Ellenbecker, Michael Lamb, Kevin Sampsell, Liz Phair, Michal Drannen, Kathi Kirby, Steffen Silvis, Mary Winzig, Steven Fidel, Georgie Honisett, Christina Smith, Amy Rabinovitz, Miriam Sontz, and Michael Powell.

None of this would have been possible without the kindness of the authors and artists who volunteered their time and energy.

Dave wishes particularly to thank everyone who has emailed him over the course of the last year and a half about PowellsBooks.news and its contents, especially those who did not use the word UNSUBSCRIBE or REMOVE in the subject line. Also Zooey and Mindy, whose patience for nonsensical ramblings sustains him.

*   *   *

This brief intermission is not brought to you by the chain store on the corner or the pill that resuscitates your sex life. This space looks like white noise and sounds like smoke.

Breathe.

About the Interviewer

When he's not talking to our store cat, Powell's Senior Executive Pet Liason talks to many of the writers and artists who visit Portland on book tours. He's a lucky bastard, he really is. The guy came from nowhere, straight out of a burger joint near the highway ramp, and, well, we honestly don't know—we think his cousin got him the job somehow.

Dave says he grew up in Massachusetts and Maine, then went to college in Montreal. Instead of spending one last frigid semester crossing the city's east side through underground tunnels wondering if the snot in his nose would defrost before he climbed the stairs to street level and again faced the cold, he moved to Portland, Oregon to complete his last nine undergraduate credits. During that four-month residence he fell in love with the flowering city and fell in love with Powell's. It seemed an unfathomably preposterous carnival of a bookstore, a ten-minute walk from his apartment.

Seven years later he moved back to Portland to stay.

iUniverse

weUniversed; you can, too. This project likely would have been impossible if not for iUniverse, the print-on-demand and electronic publisher who agreed to waive our fees, accelerate our publishing schedule, and kick in some of their share for literacy, too. iUniverse brings out-of-print titles back into circulation and works directly with authors to publish new manuscripts.

Let It Rain

Special thanks to every Portland resident, past, present, and future, for helping foster an environment where independent bookstores (and music shops, and restaurants, and so on) thrive.

Fup. Store Cat.

"Blowout," Fup said. "Triple word score."

We'd been warned. Lisa had told us how good Fup was at this game. We'd known we stood a chance of being humiliated in front of an international book-buying audience, but we agreed to play. Then Fup laid the tiles for *panoply* on her first turn, and we knew we were in trouble. Here it was, PowellsBooks.news's first time in ink, and we were being slaughtered at wordplay by a cat.

"She's taunting us," Farley complained during the intermission. "Fup is showboating."

People would understand, wouldn't they? They'd assume we were taking a dive, that we were letting the cat win. Because that would make a happier ending. Some readers might think it a bit too cute, typical Hollywood feel-good schlock, but they'd have to assume we could beat her if we tried. Wouldn't they?

Fup emerged from her dressing room after the break wearing giant pink sunglasses and her Cat Power t-shirt, cut off at the sleeves. Wild applause greeted her return to the stage. She curtsied, awash in the cheers. That entry took the wind out of us, it really did—it stole the last of our hope. We never spelled a word longer than four letters again.

<<><><><><><><>>

Comments, suggestions, words you'd like to share (there are plenty to go around), email us at interviews@powells.com.

<<><><>>

About PowellsBooks.news:

Imagine, if you will, spending your entire life in cyberspace—your *entire* life—and one day waking up on paper. "I feel like those Bhutanese archers Pico Iyer wrote about," PowellsBooks.news told friends the day of this book's publication, "the ones who'd never left Bhutan, then one day got on a plane—the first time they'd been on a plane, of course—and flew to Barcelona for the Olympics. It's a whole 'nother world.

"Paper," PowellsBooks.news marveled, "it's grittier than I'd expected. So tactile!"

PowellsBooks.news alerts subscribers to new features on our web site: staff picks, great deals (on really good books), contests unannounced elsewhere, unadvertised sales of autographed first editions, upcoming author appearances, interviews, and more. It's also where you'll find the continuing adventures of Fup and her friends. Every now and then, our overachieving newsletter introduces you to your next favorite book.

To read the latest edition of PowellsBooks.news or (bless your heart) to subscribe (it's free), point your browser to http://www.powells.com/newsletter.html or follow the link from the margin of our Home page.

<<>>

Dedication

FOR GERTIE

The Interviews

Nicholson Baker Stops Time,
But Can He Save Jiffy Pop?

◆

The author of such popular and provocative novels as *The Mezzanine* and *The Fermata*—not to mention one of the most honest, fascinating, first-person accounts of writing I know, *U & I*—Nicholson Baker found himself thrust into the national spotlight when Kenneth Starr revealed that a famous former intern had given America's President a copy of Baker's 1992 erotic classic, *Vox*. With his latest novel, *The Everlasting Story of Nory*, Baker continues to expand his literary turf, focusing his unique, digressive style on a precocious nine year old girl.

Nory, an American, is going to school in England for a year. Baker's new novel charts the adventurous course of her busy, animated mind in this strange new setting. Nory wants to be a dentist—or a designer of pop-up books, depending when you ask. She's not quite ready to obsess about career choices. No, there are plenty of equally critical ideas crowding her mind, like stuff about dung beetles and cows with pointed teeth.

Sounds like strange territory for an author forever to be associated with a national sex scandal, right? Not entirely. The leap from *Vox* to *Nory* isn't as great as it first appears.

"The riskiest thing now is something that edges on sentimentality," Baker explained. "That's the taboo. But that's also what gives it the excitement. Can you be true to a person whose life isn't damaged? Who isn't illuminating bad things about adults, but just having a fairly normal kid's life? Can you treat that complexity in a way that's interesting? I tried to, and I guess I think I did."

Nicholson Baker: It was a lot of fun to write this book [*The Everlasting Story of Nory*]. I hope that I captured some of the moral complexities of one kid's life.

Dave: Your novels are clearly fiction, but you focus so closely within the minds of your characters.

Baker: Some people just have an urge to confess things, some kind of misplaced truthfulness. You want to say the things that people haven't said—and people have said a lot of things.

Dave: What impressed me about *Vox* was the continuous motion that keeps it going, the momentum. Though obviously you didn't write it in a single sitting, the whole novel is one extended conversation.

Baker: The idea was to have one character fizzle out with a story and yet have someone else there who'd take it up, turn it, and maybe even twist it away from the intention of the person who started. It becomes antiphonal. The characters were competing with each other in a way, showing off. And of course they're both really me.

Or I'd ask my wife questions. That's the sort of thing writers do. The sordid truth is you walk out of your office and say, "Well, what would you say if I said this or that?" and your wife says, "No, I wouldn't say that." Then I tell her, "Thank you," and walk back into my office.

Dave: You mention your daughter as the source for much of the new novel.

Baker: *Nory* is based on in-depth interviews with this other human being, yes. And she was pretty tolerant about that. I wrote down what she said, then put it through my own manipulations and adjustments.

Dave: How conscious is she of all this? How old is she?

Baker: She was nine. This happened in real time. I picked her up from school, interviewed her about what happened that day, wrote a scene the next day. Picked her up, interviewed her, wrote a scene. So I didn't know how the book would end up because I didn't know how her experience in this English school would end up. She knew at the time that this was a book about her, more or less. She hasn't read it cover to cover, but she has read the parts that she more or less made up. It's a collaborative kind of work.

Dave: Was it more satisfying, working so closely with your daughter? What made you decide to try that?

Baker: The riskiest thing now isn't to do something evil or graphically sexual. The riskiest thing now is something that edges on sentimentality. That's the taboo. But that's also what gives it the excitement. Can you be true to a person whose life isn't damaged? Who isn't illuminating bad things about adults, but just having a fairly normal kid's life? Can you treat that complexity in a way that's interesting? I tried to, and I guess I think I did.

Dave: It's different than ninety-nine percent of the novels you're going to find on the shelves, and that can only be a good thing, I think.

Baker: Well, the thing that makes it similar to my earlier books…It's similar to *Vox* in that the characters made up words. They were trying to come up with a new language for a very familiar subject, and in this one, too, I was interested in the neologisms and oddities of language the character had. I would hear something interesting and write it down.

Some people who read the book seemed to think that it wasn't possible for this to be a nine year old mind, but that's because the nine year old minds we're given in fiction aren't true ones. It's not because Nory is an extraordinary character. We're given smart-aleck kids who I don't think are true to the way kids really are. The only way you can write about someone who's nine is by listening to the way they think.

Dave: You've written about protecting card catalogues from destruction and you've actively campaigned to save old books from the trash heap. It seems in that context that *Nory* is a paper or a physical record of this life, your daughter's, at this time.

Baker: It makes me unhappy when certain things change or things are superceded. Her personality…there's no way you can be nine forever. There's a sense of mortality in that each phase of a personality involves a huge loss of an earlier phase. Her vocabulary will change completely. She won't have the same words.

Card catalogues—things, too. Jiffy Pop right now feels imperiled. I always think, Thank God it's still hanging in there, even though people don't really buy it for the popcorn anymore. Maybe they never did, but now it's a nostalgia item. It was like a Pullman car when people rode the train. Now people only ride the train on special occasions. So I'm sad about Jiffy Pop.

Dave: You could hoard a whole bunch.

Baker: I do, or I *have*, actually. I have one. I packed it in a box, but it got all crumpled. Apparently there's a dish of vegetable oil in the bottom there, and once you crumple the bottom you're not going to get an even heating surface. So there are losses there, too.

I wrote a book about my obsession with Updike [*U & I*]. When you're an aspiring writer you have a certain view of the literary universe, and if you write a few more books that view is completely gone. There's no way to resurrect it. The only way to write about that accurately is when it's happening. So there is a feeling of things passing that worries me a lot. I want to stop time and get things down on paper before they've flown off like a flock of starlings.

Dave: What fascinates me about *U & I* is that you resisted your urge to go back and read all of Updike's books. That would have been the most obvious, most conventional thing to do. Being afraid that you'd come off wrong. But it's so much more interesting to read your writerly perspective rather than a scholarly perspective.

Baker: The idea is, What do you really think about a writer? You ask yourself, What do you really think about Gunter Grass? You probably have an opinion right now. But it would be completely distorted if you went back and reread *The Tin Drum*. All these little enthusiasms I've been through…is it a male thing to focus on one thing and include all the world in your tight focus, then just check that thing off, be done with it, and focus on something else? You try to include everything else in the world by implication, staying true to your focus. Then you check that subject off. I don't know if it's a good thing or not.

Dave: It seems like a perfect temperament for a writer. When you finish something, you're ready to move on to something new.

Baker: I wish that I could be like P.G. Wodehouse or something. It seems to have given him pleasure to have roughly the same plot each time. Slight variations. Like Mozart or something. Sub-dominant chords. It seems like a healthier way to approach writing, to make small variations each time. And maybe over thirty years, from the first book to the last book, there's a considerable movement. But my way seems to be to completely turn the telescope in another direction. It doesn't seem like the way a pro would do it.

Dave: Are you still worried about being a pro at this point? Still questioning yourself in that regard?

Baker: Don't you think most writers are secretly worried that they're not really writers? That it's all been happenstance, something came together randomly, the letters came together, and they won't coalesce ever again?

Dave: But you could make the opposite argument that your career has developed in a Wodehouse sort of way. You have that fascination with detail and the digressive style which lets you incorporate huge ideas in small fields. So your focus changes, but you keep the style, which itself has developed and evolved.

Baker: That's a better way to look at it.

Dave: I'm just trying to put a positive spin on it.

Baker: Well, I certainly don't feel tortured in any way.

Dave: It's been ten years since you started *U & I*. Who are you reading now?

Baker: I still very much admire Updike. I went through a Kipling jag recently. He's a really good poet. Right now I'm writing a long thing about libraries so I've been reading obscure tidbits, pieces of the story I'm telling. I've really forgotten what literature is. I carry around an anthology of English prose edited by Peacock, 1903. I find it reassuring, the onionskin. The Indians invented onionskin, according to the *Encyclopedia Britannica*, which is printed on onionskin so they should know. I'm protective of my own enthusiasms. But I've lost touch with contemporary American fiction.

Dave: You mention in *U & I* that you're protective of your reading. You want to be able to read what you want, when you want, and not be bound by obligation. Do you tend to finish everything you read or do you jump around?

Baker: I don't. I probably should finish more than I do, but there's an infinite amount of stuff to read and only a little time to read it. I think that you can have a valuable aesthetic experience having read thirty pages of a book. Often the feeling of setting out on a book is the best thing about it. So I read around.

I read a lot to make sure I'm not encroaching on someone's subject or that what I'm doing is different than someone else. It's not a good feeling to be duplicating or imitating someone. It's scary. Terrifying.

Dave: When you're writing a story, then, do you purposely distance yourself from works that have touched upon similar themes?

Baker: You usually have to confront it and make sure you won't be encroaching. It turns out most of the time you're worried about something that isn't really that close. That was one of the things that was hardest to do in *U & I*, to list the other works of nonfiction or fiction that seemed close to what I was doing. I listed *Flaubert's Parrot* and a couple of other things that were in my mind. I wanted my book to be as different as possible, but I was conscious of the fact that I was in the same territory as others who had come before.

It was hard to type that list. And sometimes when I read a book that I feel, perhaps wrongly, has been mildly influenced by *U & I*, I wish that the author had presented a similar list of immediate influences instead of recognizing only distant writers. Because you know they're lying. You have to sample the writers around you. Even if you do it like me, kind of dilettantishly, I'm still taking pH readings here and there. I'm always aware of this Milky Way of book-reviewable people who are out there. Then, of course, all writers have their heroes, like Samuel Johnson, but those are easy to cite. You're not confessing a secret.

Nicholson Baker stopped by the Powells.com Annex on April 28, 1999, prior to his appearance at the City of Books. He proved to be every bit as thoughtful in person as in his books—no small feat, as anyone who's read his work will attest.

About a year after this interview, I met Baker's editor, whose high praise for the author only reinforced my initial impression of him. I mean, he seemed to be genuinely distressed at the demise of Jiffy Pop, and I have to admit, I admire that kind of eccentric devotion. "It makes me unhappy when certain things change or things are superceded," Baker had explained. Fortunately, he's documenting his share of them before they disappear.

Midday in the Annex
with John Berendt

◆

John Berendt asks good questions. Not that this should have surprised me, but the journalist in him doesn't turn off. Before this interview, he sat across Tenth Avenue on the third floor of our City of Books location and signed first editions of *Midnight in the Garden of Good and Evil* (he knew the firsts by sight; the cloth binding is always green, he informed us, not black like the later editions). Afterwards, we walked over to the Annex and for fifteen minutes I couldn't get a question in edgewise; he wanted to know anything and everything about Internet bookselling. Finally, when he'd digested enough information about our peculiar corner of the bookselling world, we talked about his book.

Midnight in the Garden of Good and Evil, his first and (thus far) only book, is an insightful, intelligent, fun-to-read story of eccentricity and murder in Savannah, Georgia. A finalist for the Pulitzer Prize, it spent more time on the *New York Times* Bestseller list than any previous fiction or nonfiction title, ever—and that's really just the start. Savannah's annual tourist traffic has increased by 46% since Berendt's exposé was published. They've given the author two keys to the city—in case he loses the first one, I guess.

A childhood friend who now lives in Atlanta had recommended the book to me years ago, but I resisted until a couple weeks before this interview, at which point I really had no choice but to read it. I read it, finally, and I loved it; I was engrossed. Then, two days after meeting Berendt, I watched that same old friend get married—just up the coast from

Savannah. Next time, Sandy, I won't wait four years to read books you recommend.

Dave: What was the process like, creating this book?

John Berendt: I would focus on something—a person. Then I would do a chapter, approaching it as if it were an article for a magazine. It was nonfiction, writing using the fictional techniques novelists and short story writers would use: ample description, transitions, a lot of dialogue.

But I would focus on one chapter, not knowing where it was going. I didn't write it in order. In the first part of the book, each chapter more or less introduces one person. Then sometimes a character already described in his own chapter will float through to tie it together.

I lived in Savannah for five years. I was going to come down for three weeks at a time every so often, but I soon realized that I really had to be there to stumble on things, to have things happen in front of me, to hear the perfect phrase. So I went down there in '85 and stayed for five years, going back to New York rarely, just for days at a time. It unfolded. The book evolved, more or less. I didn't know how it was going to end.

One reason I didn't have an advance was that I didn't want to be committed to a timetable. I didn't know how the book was going to turn out. The story hadn't finished yet. In fact, I moved down in '85, and the trials for the murder case weren't over until June of '89. So that didn't solve itself. Then, Jim Williams [the murder suspect], six months later, he died. Well, that gave me a nice ending.

Dave: Fortuitous.

Berendt: Yes, because also he could have caused a lot of problems. He loved to cause trouble. He had a very evil wit, but he wasn't around when the book came out.

Dave: Did he read the book at all while you were working on it?

Berendt: I had read him some of the chapters. He agreed to cooperate. I said, "Well, you're not going to be able to read the book until it's published. You certainly won't have any editorial input, except through these interviews with me." So I read him four or five chapters or more, and once or twice he would say, "That was walnut, not oak," or whatever, but he never actually had any pages in his possession.

Dave: When you were reading these chapters, was this before or after he was charged with murder?

Berendt: I started after the whole thing happened. In the book, I put the murder in the middle for narrative purposes, then at the very end I explain that I've changed some things around. But when I went down and started working on it, he'd been tried already; he was in jail.

I'd met Jim Williams, the first time, in 1982. He'd been convicted six weeks prior. He was out on appeal. And we had an evening just like the first chapter when he told me stories—but he'd been convicted already of murder. That was not how I wrote it in the book.

So then I went back to New York. Three years later I decided I'd write a book, and I thought, What about Savannah? What's happening to Jim Williams? The conviction had been reversed, and he'd been tried a second time. He was in jail. I visited him in jail briefly and decided I'd write the book. The second trial was reversed, again, of course—he got out just as I was arriving again—and he was out the rest of his life. So he was available to talk to me and introduce me to people.

Dave: Joe Odom, throughout the book, constantly talks about himself as a character.

Berendt: And he did.

Dave: It must have been strange to be writing a book about all these personalities, coexisting with them, when they all knew you were writing about them.

Berendt: Everybody knew. I was there writing a book. Joe would introduce me and say, "Hey, I want you to meet Johnny B. He's here writing a book about us." People knew. And I would say, "I'm here writing a book." People thought I was very strange, that it would never sell, that no one would ever publish it.

Dave: It seems like Savannah was the perfect setting—because of all the eccentricity, certainly, but also because who other than people so eccentric would feel free to be themselves under the microscope of someone who was about to tell the world?

Berendt: They began to forget about it. They didn't see a book after two or three years. At first they might play up to me, but not later.

Dave: Were you physically taking notes in front of them?

Berendt: I always had a notebook in my back pocket. I'd duck behind the corner or, with some people, just take it out and start writing.

Dave: You were in Savannah just a few days ago to celebrate the release of the book in paperback, right?

Berendt: It was on *Good Morning America*. I go down there frequently, and they're always marvelous. They make a big fuss. They had "Breakfast in the Park with Berendt" right after the t.v. I signed books, and there was a speech by the mayor. So that was a big deal.

Some people say the book embarrasses Savannah because it's about strange people, "morally deficient people." The right wing doesn't like it. But they've given me the keys to the city twice. I've made a lot of money for the city. Basically, they like it. And it's very complimentary, even though it's about a murder.

Dave: Four years on the *New York Times* Bestseller list—in hardcover. And now it's in paperback.

Berendt: Is it going to sell, do you think?

Dave: I can't see any reason why it would stop selling, but who's left out there who hasn't read it?

It's a great book, though. I lent it to someone else here who gave it to his wife. The next day he came in and said she'd read two hundred pages. It's a story, so filled with characters. People make the Flannery O'Connor connection, largely because of Savannah, but I can't think of a novel that contains as much character. And this is nonfiction.

Berendt: They seemed to just pop out. Joe Odom had extraordinary charm. In spite of the fact that he would cut bad checks and get into business deals that lost people a lot of money, they all still loved him. Jim Williams was this marvelously malevolent character who had a very wicked sense of humor. He told stories brilliantly. The Lady Chablis is another. Those three people were extraordinary.

And then there were the minor characters who were strange: the guy with the bottle of poison, the old man who walked the invisible dog.

Dave: What didn't get in the book?

Berendt: I shoehorned practically everything in. But there was an inventor, Reuben Ware. He had invented Sara's Magic Carpet Cleaner—his wife is Sara. It would take out a spot and not leave any mark. It would also clean your windshield and do all these other things. You could gargle with it, I don't know, all sorts of things. A very funny, wonderful guy. He wrote all these little books. He was always busy. I took lots and lots of notes, and I would have written him in, but I already had an inventor, the guy with the poison, so I decided not to use him.

I asked Reuben, "If these inventions are so good, why aren't you rich?" He said [*in a rich Southern drawl*], "I've been on the doorsteps of it many times!"

Dave: What was it like to live down there?

Berendt: I loved it. It was a very comfortable, beautiful place to live. Slow-moving. I just liked it. Warm weather. I developed friends. I was in clover: I was writing, I would jog, make dinner—all the things I would do in New York. And I had a car for the first time.

Dave: Since you finished the book and it's become this massive success…well, for instance, I found a Lady Chablis web site promoting her book, *Hiding My Candy*. How have your relationships with these people evolved?

Berendt: I don't see her very much, but I did see her on Tuesday. I am in touch with the friends that I made there, whether they were in the book or not. I see Emma Kelly, The Lady of Six Thousand Songs. Lee Adler I saw in the park the other day. He's not happy with the book, though he's come around a little bit because it's made him famous. His wife hates it; there's nothing nice about her in the book. But he's become very cordial to me. Sonny Seiler, the lawyer with the bulldog, Uga—I see him occasionally.

Dave: What do you read?

Berendt: I read what friends tell me is good. This explains the book's success, partially. It got very good reviews. Good reviews will get you a readership right away, but that's it. The review or the article appears one day in a magazine or a newspaper, then it's gone. Word of mouth is a continuing phenomenon, much more powerful.

I'm reading *Memoirs of a Geisha* right now because two people told me it was wonderful, and it is. Am I right, isn't *Memoirs of a Geisha* the big summer read? It's Vintage also, and they told me that it sold five hundred thousand in hardcover and a million-five in paper. Mine has sold two and a half million in hardcover, so is there anybody left? I don't know. I'm just as happy to have sold the hardcovers. I have to sell four paperbacks in order to make what I make for one hardcover.

Dave: What about the move from magazine writing to producing a full-length book?

Berendt: I hadn't written things exactly like this in narrative. I'd written essays. But it's the same kind of style. When I worked for *Esquire* after college, the New Journalism was just then getting itself born, and that's the style that I love.

Dave: And at Harvard you wrote for the *Lampoon*. What were you doing there?

Berendt: Doggerel poetry. I wrote one short story.

Dave: It was fun, probably.

Berendt: It was.

Dave: What writing did you grow up on? What writing taught you how to write?

Berendt: I really didn't learn how to write until I was out of school. I was hired by *Esquire* because of the things I'd done for the *Lampoon*. We did a parody of *Mademoiselle,* their "July issue," that was seen by *Esquire.* That's where I learned to write.

Harold Hayes, who was the editor of *Esquire* at the time, was very particular about how the copy read. Very often we would do pieces that weren't signed, the "house-written" copy, in the voice of the magazine. Like a four-pager with photographs or drawings and you'd write the text to go with it, unsigned. He wanted it to reflect the tone and the voice of the magazine. Knowledgeable irreverence and sophistication. Very, very sharply written, getting as much information on the page as possible—with a certain attitude. We really worked very hard.

Also, he realized that the short bits of copy in a magazine were the most important because someone could thumb through a magazine and only read the short text and captions just to get an idea of the titles. They might put the magazine down meaning to come back to it but never look at it again. Yet in their mind, later, they'd think they'd read it. We sometimes spent two weeks on the titles. It was very carefully done.

Dave: I read a story about the movie adaptation of your book that said the producers were going to make the main character a lawyer instead of a writer.

Berendt: Oh, that was just one of the changes they considered. I got a phone call one day and they said, "Guess who's going to play you?" I said, "Who?" And they said, "Jodie Foster." They wanted Jodie Foster to have an affair with Joe Odom. It just got completely out of control.

Dave: In an interview, you thanked Clint Eastwood for taking time from his busy schedule to make a ten million dollar commercial for your book.

Berendt: I did say that. I think Clint may have seen it, and I'm not sure he would have been too happy. I was just hoping that the movie would come out while the book was still in hardcover, and it did. But I had very little to do with it. I didn't want my name on it. It wasn't my product.

Dave: What do you want to do now?

Berendt: I want to write another book that's as much fun to write as this one. I don't have any illusion that the next book I write will be anywhere near as successful—it's impossible. So what I really want is for the book to be engrossing and fun and exciting. And it would have some of the same elements. It would have a very good story with some suspense in it. Surprises—I love surprises. Very unusual, compelling characters. A place that creates an atmosphere. It could be a building or a farm or a jail, not necessarily a city. And humor, that's the tough part. It has to be something that I enjoy doing.

John Berendt visited Powell's City of Books on July 14, 1999. Good thing he came when he did because if I'd seen the movie adaptation of *Midnight in the Garden* before reading his book, I might not have given it a chance. It's not that I don't appreciate Sandy's taste in books—in fact, we share many of the same favorites—but it's not often I have time to read books unrelated to work. I'm not complaining, just saying. But next time I'll read what Sandy tells me, I really will.

David Brancaccio:
Off the Air and On the Road

$\blacklozenge$

"Ten trips sprinkled over sixteen months of a busy work schedule... It would be a pilgrimage to see what other folks were doing with their money as the century closed with a boom and to explore those possibilities in three dimensions, not just as data on one of my flat market screens. A pilgrimage, because you hear stories and because strange things happen."

From Chapter 1 of *Squandering Aimlessly*

I don't think nearly enough about money. Which is to say, I feel guilty about the fact that I never think about it if I don't have to. I don't read finance books; in fact, I don't know that I'd even been to that section of our store in the first year I worked at Powell's. I did take Microeconomics second semester freshman year, but the class met at 9 a.m., and if anything is clear about those years of my life it's that I've retained almost nothing that happened before noon.

David Brancaccio hosts Public Radio International's *Marketplace*, which I'd never heard, of course—it being about, I correctly assumed, money. But someone gave me a copy of *Squandering Aimlessly* about a month before David's visit, and I'd read only a couple chapters when I knew I wanted to see if he'd stop by a bit early to talk about the book.

Dave: Your book, in many ways, seemed eerily targeted toward me.

David Brancaccio: You have one of these consumption problems, do you?

Dave: No, not at all, actually. But I do have a problem being comfortable with money, and the consequence of that is that I've spent almost no time thinking about what I'd do with it were I ever to have some. Since I was old enough to make money I've wanted to be a writer, so I haven't spent much time worrying what I'd do with a bunch of cash. It's never been much of an issue.

But now here I am, I'm thirty, and I have a business card that says "Web Producer." I have a paycheck, suddenly, and benefits. I work for an independent bookstore so I'm not exactly raking it in hand over fist, but there's this booming job market out there populated by executives barely my age offering insane amounts of money to people with practically no experience in the field. It's very strange to suddenly find myself here.

Brancaccio: You are the poster child for this book. It's funny because when you get the wrong demographic for this book, they say, "I never had any questions about money. I just wanted more of it."

I got a letter at *Marketplace* a few months ago from an attorney in Maine, my home state, who didn't like the notion of public radio giving up a half-hour a night to—quote, "business news." His argument was that the whole world is reporting business and public radio should be a refuge from all of it. He asked me, "Don't you realize there's more to life?"

And I'm chuckling because he has no idea that my undergraduate major was in History and African Studies, that I don't have a M.B.A. I share his ironic detachment from this stuff. But the letter also made me wonder, Who is this guy that he can have a job completely outside the sphere of money? Is he independently wealthy? Is he a hermit?

Money doesn't just go away. Even if you're an artist, you have to know something about marketing. My brother went to the California

Institute of Art. They teach a whole class there in marketing your paintings and how to caption them so they sell.

Dave: You decided to structure the book around a series of trips. It's not a travel book, per se, but it owes as much to that genre as it does to the titles in our Personal Finance section.

Brancaccio: I wondered how I could come to grips with some of these things. I asked myself, "Is there a way to approach money on your own terms?" And I also thought I needed to get street-smart about this.

I have parents who took us traveling all the time. We talked about politics and we talked about history. We never talked about money. Hard work, sure, but not personal finance. How could I make up for that? I realized that one cool way would be to take a road trip.

Marketplace, where I work, has no windows, not a single one. It's like working in a submarine. I needed to get out of that place and be a reporter. If you stay in the hermetically sealed capsule, reporting from our dark bunker, it all becomes abstract, and that's exactly what we're not supposed to be doing on public radio, divorcing all this stuff from its human component.

Some people say the economy is booming. For others, it isn't. Well, how does that play out in people's lives? And if suddenly you have a surplus, some savings, is selling out the only thing you can do?

Growing up, I read a lot of narrative travel. Paul Theroux. I have a warm place in my heart for those types of stories. Because of my job I'm given practically every personal finance book that's written, and lots of them are good, but where they have a failing, for me, is that so many of them are bullet points and spread sheets. I don't retain information that way. I retain through narrative. I remember stories and folklore. So I wanted to go out and find the folklore about money.

Dave: You've probably noticed from walking through our office that Powell's isn't a very business-like environment, at least not in the traditional sense. I think most of us here are in the same boat: money is a fact of life, and yet we're awkward around it. We feel like there's something wrong with it, or certainly that there's something wrong about striving for it. I'm not sure that many of us have even defined exactly what's wrong with having money, but that's the point. We don't even like to think about it.

Brancaccio: Looking around, I think there'd be a consensus here that you don't want to be materialistic. You don't want a raise just to buy more *stuff*. So you think, I don't want a lot of extra money because then I'd have to worry about all the stuff that would imply. But many of us haven't thought through to the point where we ask, "If it's not stuff that money could get you, what would it get you?" It turns out there are wider possibilities.

Real estate, for instance. But I always worried about real estate, that it turned you into a creep—at the point that you bought the house, you'd turn into Ward and June Cleaver. You suddenly become middle class and adopt suburban values. That's not what I found when I went to the place where it would have shown up if it ever did, Levittown on Long Island, the cradle of suburbia. For better or worse, there are problems in Levittown, but there's a real community. Home ownership allows you to connect with other people in a way that a rental doesn't.

And the chapter that I liked the most, reporting it, was when I asked, "Is it really irresponsible to use money to follow a long-held yearning?" That's what I had done with money once. We used our savings to quit our jobs and move to England so I could become a big-time foreign correspondent—which was great, except that *Marketplace* paid me two hundred fifty dollars a week in American funds and the exchange rate was terrible. The money disappeared in nine months.

A financial advisor would have had a heart attack if I'd walked in and said, "This is the most money we've ever seen and we're going to dispense with it in nine months. No, we don't own a house. Actually, we have no net worth except for this, but we're going to follow this lark in England."

But you know what? It was an investment. There's no way I'd have this job if I hadn't taken that risk. So it did have a return on investment that turned out to be very high.

Dave: In the book, that's the chapter where you visit the country music school in Texas.

Brancaccio: I met people who'd quit good jobs in medicine and advertising to pick banjo. Were they insane? No, they weren't. You should have seen their faces. They're really digging it. And they don't all go to Nashville with their new Associates degree in commercial music. Some do. But some leave the school much more centered about their place in the universe, what they're doing, what their goals are, and satisfied, knowing they've done something they really wanted to do—in this case, play.

If you think of money as only buying a sport utility vehicle or a really nice camera, you say, "Why do I need more money? I'll turn into one of those people who just buys stuff." But there are wider possibilities.

And if you don't think this through, other people's agendas take over. If you walk into a meeting with a financial advisor unprepared, they'll sell you whatever they want, whereas if you tell that advisor, "I really want to spend a year in China. This is how much money I think I'll need. How can I save this much? How long will it take?" that person is much more likely to help you achieve a meaningful goal.

Maybe it's just that you want a bigger house. Regardless, I think it's self-evident that money is power. I got to age thirty-six before I'd ever considered this stuff. People who are uncomfortable with the notion of waking up and reading *The Wall Street Journal*…well, that doesn't have to happen.

Dave: You don't say anywhere in the book, "This is how to make the most money." Instead, you present the arguments for and against using money in a variety of ways. For me, that's the value: you present various options in an objective way so readers can decide for themselves which is best suited to them. You can invest in socially responsible companies, you can start your own business, you can buy a house, you can go to Vegas or blow it all at the mall.

For instance, you write toward the end of the book about a man from Idaho who sells his business and spends the money on a sailboat, which, taken out of context, might seem like a short-sighted use of a big wad of cash. But you conclude,

> David's boat passes what I am finally realizing is the important test for a surplus: he can answer "yes" if asked if he expects his use of his money to have a lasting positive impact on the rest of his life…[The boat] is something he has wanted for a very long time and is an expression of who David Hunt is.

Brancaccio: It isn't about what *I* would say. What I would do with the money isn't what you should do with it. You don't need to ask experts what the right thing to do with money is; you should sit down and discuss your options with the people involved, your wife, whomever. Yes, a 401K plan, on paper, is a great deal for lots of people, but I have no idea if you have something eating away at you that you just really want to do. I just can't know that.

Dave: There's also a theme of prudence in the book.

Brancaccio: This is supposed to be a great golden age—again, if you're lucky enough—and yet people are not saving. They think it will get even more golden, and they're borrowing against the bigger paychecks they expect to be ahead.

But you don't know what's going to happen. The economy is looking great—the Dow was up about three hundred points when I checked last—so we never need emergency money for anything because everything is just fine, right? That situation worries me.

If it's not self-evident what you should be doing with money, hold onto it. It's no crime to save it. You know that when the whole thing comes tumbling down *Marketplace* is going to be doing a million stories about people who feel cheated, people who lost a lot, people who were heavily invested in volatile investments and needed their money quick, which is a crazy position to put yourself in.

There's a whole industry that's risen up, inasmuch as the market is a participant sport—it's not like *watching* a hockey game, it's like *playing* a hockey game, and people want to play at home. CNBC is merging, in terms of style and diction, with ESPN. Yet there's credible research, controversial but pure review, that suggests the more you trade, the worse you do.

Dave: Also, the more you know, the worse you do. You mention a Harvard study in the book that concluded, "Investors who listen, watch, or read business news make less money than those who don't."

Brancaccio: But it's the same principle: the more the media covers it moment to moment, the more likely you are to act moment to moment. So what do you do? When you hear everything is going to hell in a hand basket, you sell, and you when you hear everything is looking great, you buy—which is pretty much the exact opposite of what you should do.

Dave: Powell's is an independent bookstore, but Powells.com operates in the e-commerce world. In many ways, it's an entirely contradictory position.

About a year ago, an ad guy from a major worldwide service provider came in here and insulted us to our faces, basically, because we told him, no, forty thousand dollars a month for banner ads on his browser seemed a bit steep without any kind of guarantee that the people seeing those ads would buy a single book—and that was the smallest ad package he was offering. He was wearing a suit, and I think we threw him off with our shorts and sandals, but mostly he was put off by our refusal to simply hand over the money. I don't think most e-companies think twice before spending that kind of cash.

We're always dealing with young Internet businesses, and seven out of ten of them have very little idea what they're doing. They just got millions from a venture capitalist but they're completely unorganized. It's painfully obvious, more so when we have to work with them in some capacity. Some catch up quickly, but it's not a perspective that lends much confidence in the industry. It's exciting to watch all this happen from the inside, but it's a little bit frightening, too.

Brancaccio: Maybe Powell's has the last laugh. The one thing that can't happen to you is that your share price evaporates overnight. Yes, a lot of these e-companies, they say, "Oh, I'm so liquid now." They want to pay for anything. But someone's going to notice that these business plans don't produce a profit in the foreseeable future.

Still, the e-commerce space isn't going to go away. The revolution has happened, and it's not going away. But the texture of it is going to radically change. It would be very cool if the clever strategy in e-commerce is to be a privately held company that doesn't actually have to suffer when the day of reckoning comes.

Or maybe there is no big day of reckoning. Maybe there's lots of little bubbles that pop on different days. On the other hand, it seems like it's a little overdone.

The example that I've often given is this: Edward Chancellor wrote a book about the history of financial speculation [*Devil Take the Hindmost: A History of Financial Speculation*], published just last year, in which he talks about the wave of financial speculation that built the U.S. railroads in the nineteenth century. All these people invested in the railroads, so they built the railroads. And they all went bust. Those investors—*boom!*—they lost their shirts. But those investments built the railroads which built the country.

It's not that speculation is bad—and it could be that this wave of speculation is building an incredible new infrastructure which will persist—but woe is the investor who got in early and with the wrong companies. That's going to be the problem.

Dave: Is there a business book similar to yours, or even completely different, which you'd recommend?

Brancaccio: Well, the one that's similar but certainly generationally different is *Investment Biker* by Jim Rogers. He gets on a motorcycle with—and this is his quote, not mine—"with a woman half his age," and they go cruising around the world. As he confronts different things on motorcycle, different cultures, different countries, he talks about his philosophy for figuring out what a good company is in which to invest and also about emerging markets and so forth.

Travel is a good vehicle to explain something because of its narrative power. Outside the realm of personal finance, Bill Bryson taught me an awful lot about the Appalachian Trail [in *A Walk in the Woods*], as funny as he is, and as impressionistic and hapless. It's a wonderful way to communicate ideas, the travel adventure.

Peter Bernstein has a really good tome about risk called *Against the Gods*. It teaches you probability in a very compelling way and puts it in a historical context.

And the Motley Fools are fantastic because they really do show you that personal finance and investing isn't that complicated. We differ a little bit in theory, but the Fools, in their own way, are really useful.

Dave: Toward the end of the book, you visit a "retirement campus" affiliated with the University of Arizona. You describe it as a community "for the sort of folks who might have 'emeritus' in their title or for artists, writers, and other interesting professional people." You write, "It will be assisted living for people with active minds who want to continue using their minds in retirement in a Medicare-approved setting…but money alone won't get you in…people who have lived the kind of lives that were long on accumulating a surplus and short on community involvement may have trouble getting in."

It occurred to me while I was reading that chapter that after high school and college, when we're finished padding our resume with French Club and all the rest, in most lines of work there's very little incentive to be a good person in the community, other than whatever personal satisfaction it may bring.

It seems interesting, first, that a university would make this effort to harness the experience and wisdom of older generations for their students, but also, that they would judge applicants largely on the basis of community involvement. It sounds like an interesting idea.

Brancaccio: Well, they've started building the houses, though they've changed some of the structure since I wrote the book. It was more co-op in nature when I was there—you'd pay a co-op fee and you wouldn't have to mow your lawn or cook your own meals and the rest—but people putting down money for those houses wanted to cook their own meals, thank you very much, so the initial plan has evolved somewhat.

But as to your broader point, yes, this is one of the great American tragedies. You go to many a suburb and there is a real lack of community involvement. There are no seeming rewards for getting involved. You have houses built that only present a garage door to the street, and it's very clear what that says.

Dave: That's a big issue here in Portland, actually. They're called "snout houses," and there's an ongoing political debate as to whether contractors should be permitted to build them.

Brancaccio: In the charity chapter, I go to a town that hasn't had a business relocate there in twenty years, Hawthorne, Nevada. They also have a terrible teen pregnancy problem. And meanwhile, they're trying to win the All-America City competition! You have to ask, "How?" Well, it turns out that it's civic involvement they're promoting. The citizens are getting out of the house into public spaces, and they're talking, trying to figure out how they're going to solve their problems. In the end, they don't win the contest, but what they gain in the process of organizing their campaign is pure social capital. They're building community.

It's true: money is the scorecard. There's no scorecard for civic involvement. It's a huge problem. For example, parents who feel like they don't ever have to get involved in the public schools, yet they complain bitterly about the public schools. At what point are people going to make the connection?

As for retirement, I don't know about you, but I really never could fathom it. It seemed morbid, like death, like writing your will. And also, my parents haven't retired yet, so why would I think about it, right? But you'll never save for it until you've at least thought it through. What will you need to get there?

It's not necessarily a profound point, but it was for me, when I realized there are two phases of retirement. There's the groovy, wonderful phase when you can do all the stuff your job had always kept you from doing.

And there's the part when you get infirm. There's an old folks home in all of our futures in that sense. How much will that cost? How much will it cost to get there? At my present level of savings, do I get there? The answer in my case was "No way."

David Brancaccio visited Powell's City of Books (for the first time) on February 28, 2000. He asked for a picture of the storefront sign bearing his name to send down east to his parents in Maine, so we had some fun playing with the cover of his book and an actual photo of our main entrance. (You won't find it in this book, but it's there on our web site, I swear.) Oh, the joys of Photoshop 5.0!

Susie Bright's Recipes for Fantasy Revelation

◆

Susie Bright is in demand these days, writing weekly columns on the Net, editing both the *Best American Erotica* series and the annual *Herotica* collections, making public appearances around the country, and, of course, writing books. Her newest, *Full Exposure*, attempts to capture the meaning and the power of erotic expression. By challenging the status quo in most aspects of our public lives, her book raises important questions about the way we choose to live and communicate.

Usually, we conduct these interviews in person. This time, however, due to an ill-timed bout of the flu, we tried something a little different: a back and forth conversation via email. We've cleaned up the typos and creative punctuation at no extra charge.

Dave: For lack of a more subtle way to start this correspondence, I'm going to tell you about my experience this morning on the bus.

I was finishing your book on the way to work—I take the bus—and you know how people are always curious about what the person next to them is reading? Well, the bus was full, it was rush hour, and I'd been reading for about five minutes when I turned a page to see, in bold print at the top of the left hand page:

IX. Make a recipe for fantasy revelation.

Masturbate.

I thought, Okay, I really should close the book and read the last few pages when I get to work. The woman sitting next to me is going to think I'm some kind of freak. But that would have gone against everything you'd been saying in the previous hundred fifty pages—basically, to speak openly and honestly about sex and eroticism—so I kept the book open and read on. But I couldn't help wondering what the woman next to me must have been thinking.

Susie Bright: I love that you're reading my book on the bus! You can't really predict what the young woman was thinking, and it was certainly a harmless way to have a sexual question posed in a public place. She might be running out to find a copy right now!

I think a lot of people bring their favorite book onto public transit and hope someone will be nosy and look over their shoulder. It's activism for the shy!

Dave: I do find it's an interesting experiment, actually. I'm always reading different books for this job—everything from children's books to, well, yours—and the reactions from people are interesting.

Another book I was reading this week was Barbara Kingsolver's collection of essays, *High Tide in Tucson*. One passage jumped out at me in relation to what I was reading in your book. Citing the contradictions inherent in raising a girl in contemporary society, Kingsolver writes:

> The only subject more loaded with contradictions [than freedom] is the related matter of sex, which—in the world we've packaged for adolescents—is everywhere, visibly, the goal, and nowhere allowed.

Bright: When her book came out, we were both on tour, and simultaneously invited to speak at an independent bookseller's *breakfast* in Oakland. I had to go on first, at *eight a.m.*, and, of course, talk about sex.

She hugged me afterwards and told me how brave I was. I think the audience was brave to eat that Hilton breakfast, for that matter. I'm sure we all would have rather been in bed, having sex, or at least a decent cup of coffee.

As for young people, they have been turned into the *fetish du jour*. Even the word *children* sounds vaguely pornographic these days, as they are alternately idolized for their nubile forms, vilified for creating sexual chaos, and patronized as the ultimate victims, the gossamer innocents who engender sexual criminality by their very existence.

Dave: Another quote from your book: "Our culture uses sex in the most cynical way to 'sell' anything—even though we blanch when sex is presented simply, or sold for itself."

It's true, sex sells everything. This isn't a new concept, but it seems lately to have reached absurd proportions. Yet the definitions of what is sexy seem hardly to have expanded at all—at least in the mainstream media. Is popular culture providing better images these days? Everybody on t.v. and in the movies and magazines is still unreasonably thin, fit, and wealthy. That's still what we're supposed to believe makes you popular and attractive.

Bright: I actually think the popular youth culture is more diverse. The Gap uses butch girls and chunky models sometimes. *Vogue* and *Rolling Stone* play around with cultural diversity as the sexy new thing now, too. The image of the nerd is now sexy. There are now sexy clothes in over size fourteen, with Emme as their superstar spokeswoman.

But that's just advertising getting smart, finding new skin to press, new angles to get the money out of your pocket. What's shocking is that nobody mentions that *none* of these clothes will actually *make* you sexy, and no amount of buying *anything* will make you a successful lover, a creative erotic person, a hot babe, or anything else.

Dave: Regarding tolerance: All categorical divisions of people—hetero/homo, black/white, male/female, Jew/Christian—are drawn by the differences between us. Inevitably, people wind up rationalizing their own lifestyle and, at times, defending it at the expense of alternatives. What if, instead, we learned to celebrate the similarities, the passions we all share (albeit each in our own unique way)? Are humans simply too defensive to think this way?

Bright: Oh, I don't think it's hopeless at all, if that's what you're saying. I mean, just look at the crowd who came to see me in Portland…they were all ages and types and sexual points of view. There are plenty of people who have learned the thrill of tolerance and have no inclination to turn back!

Dave: In Chapter Fourteen, you write, "Why are so many spiritual movements obsessed with eradicating the sexual?…repression of the body is prerequisite to subordination."

To me, that passage strikes at the heart of the whole book. Sex is free expression. It's a language we all speak. It demands (and rewards) creativity. Sexuality offers power. Power leads to control.

"Sexuality is the soul of the creative process and erotic expression of any kind is a personal revolution," you write. Exactly! But revolutions, of any kind, are not popular with authority.

Bright: Yes, it's too bad everyone can't take their control and/or victim fantasies and just act them out in a nice little S/M scenario, where it would come to a tidy and consensual end upon afterglow!

Dave: You explain, "I like any group that calls for a reassessment of my assumptions." Well, this is essentially the threat you pose to authority.

Bright: Yeah, that's me. The status quo has always given me the creeps.

Dave: Plenty of couples have trouble communicating openly about issues of sexuality. What's a good way to break the ice? Where should they start?

Bright: May I offer my book, or even my web site, as an ice breaker? I just got interviewed today by someone who said they were reading my book on an airplane, and their seatmate finally couldn't hold herself back and just burst into a conversation. I think it's great to use books, movies, art—all our cultural obsessions—to begin a conversation, to feel someone out.

Dave: Have you read Nicholson Baker's novel, *Vox*? I was reminded of it by the passage you wrote about the lack of words we have to express sex—the part in his novel where the characters share their own made-up words to describe a woman masturbating.

Bright: Oh, yes, I not only read it, I began a friendship with him based upon it. We had all sorts of arguments about what kind of vocabulary sex calls for. I like made-up words, I really do. The best thing about language is its reinvention.

Dave: In one of my favorite parts of the book, you talk about the importance of choosing the right words for an audience when talking about sex: *cock* or *penis*, *hard-on* or *erection*. And you give an example from your own experience when you learned that choosing the wrong words could immediately alienate the person you were talking to, whichever words happened to make them uncomfortable.

Besides the fact that this is a great point, I had to laugh because it reminded me of a girl I had a crush on when I was eleven or twelve years old. But ultimately, I thought she was…I don't know what I thought she was, but I was really turned off by the fact that she used the word *bum* to describe her ass. Even *butt* would have been better than *bum*.

Bright: Ha! Was she British? Yes, I know the way people can just completely turn off to you if they think you use a sexual word that either grosses them out or seems too pretentious.

Dave: You write:

> Think about other controversial or sometimes painful aspects of life, and you don't see people so upset about the words we use to describe them. No one says, "I can't abide the word *war*," or rails that "the word *torture* is so cruel on the tongue," or proclaims, "I don't allow anyone to say *taxes* in my home."

Yes. You still can't say the *f* word on the radio. And yet, to use an example from the heart of popular culture, Dave Matthews sings in "Crash" about "coming" into the "you" of the song, telling her to hike up her skirt—and it's on the radio about twice an hour.

Every minute of every day, we're bombarded with lustful, erotic imagery. So why can't we talk about it publicly? And do you have any advice for people who want to talk about it, but can't break through the fear of what people will think of them?

Bright: Oh, I like that song. It is the world being shown when a woman lifts her skirt. I appreciate the metaphors as well as the plain facts. As for advice for the shy, I just think a little inspiration and courage is called for. You don't have to get on a soapbox; you just have to take a tiny chance with one person, a friend, or maybe another seatmate on the airplane!

What's the result of *never* speaking your mind? That's what we ought to be concerned about.

As for other stuff, please let people know loud and clear that I would welcome them at my web site, www.susiebright.com, and they can also email me at susie@susiebright.com and get an actual reply!

I began sending emails back and forth with Susie Bright prior to her appearance in Portland on September 29, 1999—which proved to be a strange way to spend a morning in the office. I'd be typing up a book review or testing links on new site pages when an email would arrive in my Inbox, at which point I was expected to think about sex again. Off, on, off, on.

   "What'd she say?" Darin would ask, seeing me click into Outlook and open the message. I'd read it out loud. Miel would laugh; Farley might make some kind of smart, sharp quip. Then I'd put my headphones back on and try to think of another question.

Bill Bryson Is More Popular Than The Beatles

◆

Everything, it seems, is interesting to Bill Bryson. The marvel is that he can make it all interesting to us—three billion year old fossilized organisms off the western coast; a giant lobster on the side of a highway; empty, forbidding spaces…

"It's just like when you hear a great story in a bar," he explained, "an anecdote that you want to rush right home and relate to other people. You want to spread the word."

Eighty percent of Australia's plants and animals exist nowhere else in the world. A 19th century naturalist caught two rare pig-footed bandicoots—in time, he grew hungry and ate them, and no one has seen a pig-footed bandicoot since. Among the first round of convicts Great Britain exiled to Australia was a man who had been jailed for stealing twelve cucumber plants.

In a Sunburned Country introduces Australia, a giant, mostly barren continent in the Indian Ocean populated by eighteen million people, or, as Bryson points out, less people than are born each year in China. Like the rest of his writing, the new book is informative, funny, and almost impossible to put down.

Dave: I've been devouring your books for the last month or so, but I saved *In a Sunburned Country* for last. I just finished a couple days ago.

Bill Bryson: I have a particular affection for it. In a really strange way I feel as if I've become an evangelist for Australia. Just in the sense that I went there and everything I discovered was new to me. It's just like when you hear a great story in a bar, an anecdote that you want to rush right home and relate to other people. You want to spread the word.

I wound up feeling like that about Australia. Stories about Burke and Wills ["the antipodean equivalents of Lewis and Clark," Bryson calls them in *In a Sunburned Country*, "which is perhaps a little curious since their expedition accomplished almost nothing, cost a fortune, and ended in tragedy"], that kind of thing. I just thought, God, I've never heard of any of this!

Learning about the country became almost an obsession, except it was a really pleasant one. Writing this book was a pleasure. I set off without any certainty that I was going to have enough information and stories— stuff to fill a book. Pretty quickly I realized there was so much more to Australia than I'd expected and there wouldn't be a problem at all.

Dave: The format of *A Walk in the Woods* was largely determined by the Appalachian Trail, obviously, though once you started the hike you got away from your initial plan a bit. And you originally wrote the pieces that eventually became *I'm a Stranger Here Myself* for a weekly column in a British newspaper, so that shaped the style and structure of the book. But you went to Australia without any particular agenda?

Bryson: The first time I went there was in 1992. I went to a literary festival in Melbourne. After that I was sent there on book tours and I went once or twice on magazine assignments. Little by little I was getting more experience with the country. I realized pretty early on that I really liked this place.

By the time I came to write the book, I knew there would be quite a bit to it, but once I started really looking into it and gathering material, I was just astounded how much extra stuff there was. Things like the *Batavia* business, the shipwreck on the West Australia coast. Here I was driving up the west coast, and I had nothing in particular to write about. I'd already talked a lot about wide open spaces and what it's like to be in the middle of nowhere. I had nothing really to fill out that chapter. Then I stopped in this little maritime museum in a little rinky-dink town and found a whole story of slaughter, an incredible tale. It was like that everywhere I went. The material just seemed to be there, provided for me. It felt very abundant. There was always plenty to choose from.

Dave: I think your fans might argue that you simply see stories where others might not. Your style lends itself to that kind of casual observation, finding amazing anecdotes and histories in everyday events and regular people. Reading the book, it feels like you could have written a couple hundred more pages.

Bryson: I really could have. There was plenty more to go on if I wanted to talk in more detail about the history of exploration in Australia, for instance, or how the Aborigines got there. I was throwing stuff out and cutting back. At one point, I was tempted to just run on more, and really it was because I was on such a tight deadline that I had to restrict myself. The publisher was adamant that I produce the manuscript by the first week in January or they couldn't guarantee that the book would be published in time for the Olympics.

I don't think the Olympics are necessarily what is going to make or break this book, but I did feel that if the book came out next year, after the Olympics had come and gone, Australia would seem like last year's story. You have to be ahead of that, rather than behind it.

Dave: A lot of it really resonated for me because I'd just been to New Zealand for the first time. I was there in April.

Bryson: What did you think of it?

Dave: I loved it. One habit we share, apparently, is reading local newspapers when traveling. I got addicted to the local papers when I was in New Zealand. I read them every day, practically cover to cover.

One story in particular, my favorite, was about a parrot who was being evicted from a local pub by the city's health inspectors because they decided the cigarette smoke would be very bad for its health. And the locals were up in arms about it. They said, "The parrot is neurotic when he's not here! He's going to be miserable!"

Are newspapers a major source of material for you, or are they more a source of entertainment?

Bryson: Both, really. I learn a lot from newspapers, but mostly I was reading for the pleasure of it. There's just a feeling when you open a newspaper—this happens often in foreign countries—when you realize these are great stories but you know they're never going to make it anywhere overseas. You're so glad to be there when it's happening.

I find myself mostly flipping through the political stuff when I first arrive in a country, but I was in Australia for sustained enough periods that I was becoming engrossed in everything, as if I was trying to track the whole nation. I don't know to what extent that was really useful for material, but it made me feel as if I was slowly coming to grips with this very large and unwieldy country.

Dave: Australia is so far away. You talk at the end of the book, upon leaving, about the sadness of knowing that this whole nation will go on existing and you won't get to be a part of it. There really is a sense that it's another world.

Bryson: To an outsider, Australia and New Zealand are very similar. The experience you had would have been much the same in Australia except for one important factor, and that's that Australia's landscape is almost extraterrestrial.

New Zealand, most of the time, is recognizable as a part of the planet, whereas you go into the Australian outback and it looks like Mars. You have this immensity, this emptiness. You're driving, for instance, and you stop the car to get out, and first of all, the heat hits you—you're not ready for that—and the scale of everything around you, the silence, and the color of the earth, the barrenness of it—it does really feel as if somehow you've been transported to another planet where you are able, miraculously, to breathe their thin atmosphere.

Dave: After the gold rush in the 1850's, the British gave up trying to use Australia as a penal colony. Too many people wanted to go to Australia, suddenly. But it seemed strange to me, with all that emptiness and desolation—as if because a tiny portion of the land mass was now appealing they should just write off the whole project. Did they just not want to make the effort to bring the prisoners into the outback?

Bryson: Australia had been a preposterously undesirable place where nobody wanted to go—no one wanted to be posted there, convicts didn't want to be sent there—and suddenly the whole world was trying to get there. Word started to come back of these fabulous gold finds, and there was the same greed factor as in California. All this happened very quickly. Convicts were escaping and vanishing into the mass of people in the gold fields. Before that, there was no real reason to flee; there was nothing to flee *to*. So in terms of the logistics, the prisons became unsustainable.

Dave: Among the strange, almost unbelievable stories you relate are those of the British prisoners exiled to the other side of the world. One man was sent there for stealing twelve cucumber plants. Other stories are outrageously coincidental and funny, like when Captain Cook landed in Sydney and the French explorers, who were on a two-year expedition, sailed into Botany Bay a few hours behind him only to discover that the land had been claimed, so they graciously turned their boats around, sank somewhere at sea, and were never heard from again.

Another explorer had previously sailed between Australia and New Guinea without realizing he was passing an enormous undiscovered continent. There's so much colorful, strange history.

Bryson: That's my point exactly. There was so much. You wouldn't think that a country of just eighteen million people—a very small population base with which to generate history and anecdote and incident—and a relatively short history, a couple hundred years, would be so amazingly productive. But if an Australian story wasn't amazing in some way, I didn't need it for the book because there are so many that *are* amazing. So much of the history is bound up with amazing coincidences like La Pérouse and his ships arriving right after Cook gets there.

Dave: Contemporary stories, too. I think it's right at the beginning that you mention Harold Holt, the prime minister who went for a swim offshore and disappeared forever. Later in the book you discover that the memorial Australians dedicated to him was a municipal swimming pool!

Bryson: I love that!

Dave: Who are these people? That's so bizarre.

Bryson: I can't fit that one into any sort of pattern. Australians have a rich sense of humor and they're very much appreciative of irony, so it's extremely unlikely that something so lacking in irony like that would ever happen. It was totally out of character—unless they did it on purpose.

Dave: You're originally from Iowa, and so much of Australia seems reminiscent of the Midwest. The Big Lobster on the side of the highway, for instance. On one hand, things seem very familiar. On the other hand, you find a former deputy prime minister hocking his autobiography from a card table in a city market, and you just have to shake your head.

Bryson: That's what I find so mesmerizing about it. It's a contrast between the wildly exotic, things you can't see anywhere else—nowhere else in the world are you going to see kangaroos in a natural state, or even just animals hopping across the landscape; everything you look at reminds you that you're in an exotic place; the way the sun shines, that particular intensity—and at the same time all the infrastructure is familiar and well-known. It's not remotely taxing to be there. You know how to read the menu and order. You know how to read the road signs. Communication is at no stage a difficulty. All the comforts you have at home are easily duplicated. It's like going to another planet without giving up the comfortable bed.

Dave: Perth, in particular, seems fascinating to me—on an isolated continent, a major city which, itself, is completely isolated from the rest of the country. What is Perth like compared to the rest of Australia?

Bryson: Very much less different than you would imagine. When you're there, there's no sense of it being really remote. If you didn't know that it was such an isolated place, it would never occur to you. You could be a hundred fifty miles from Adelaide or Melbourne.

It's only when you get to talking to the people that you realize, for instance, when they have a long weekend, there's nowhere for them to go. They have a very nice, congenial city, but there's really nowhere else to go. They can drive out into the desert, but you'd only get so far before you'd have to turn around and go home because you have to be back at work on Tuesday.

One thing I didn't write about in the book—I really didn't think about it until later—you really appreciate Perth's isolation when you fly into it. You spend hours and hours crossing these endless deserts, or hours crossing an empty ocean if you're coming from the other direction, but if you cross the mainland particularly, it's just emptiness, Death Valley forever. Then suddenly there's the city clustered at the edge of the sea, almost as if the desert is nudging it off the continent. It's such a bizarre thing. It's all red and barren for thousands of miles, then suddenly there are golf courses and a city.

Dave: You write about the Aborigines, their ancient history and the irreconcilable differences of their worldview. It's not hard to imagine why integrating them into white Australian culture would be near impossible, yet in many ways the Australians' failings in that regard have been so blatant that it's hard to understand. Until the sixties, most Aborigines parents didn't even have legal custody of their children; in many cases, their children were simply taken away and moved to foster homes.

Today, Australia seems like a thriving, multicultural place—you note that one of every three residents of Sydney was born in another country—but only about thirty years ago, thousands of books were banned and because of the White Australia policy it was next to impossible for anyone of non-European descent to settle there.

Bryson: It wasn't really until the seventies that immigrants started coming in large numbers. Certainly in the sixties it would have been more difficult for a Vietnamese to immigrate, for instance, than a Belgian or Irish or Italian.

Dave: How did that change occur? Why did it take so long?

Bryson: In a sense, it's like asking, "Why didn't America have a successful civil rights movement until the sixties?" Sometimes history doesn't move so fast. There isn't really a plausible or satisfactory answer.

What is amazing is that there was this remarkable transformation. Australia went from being a pink-skinned, sunburned, Britannic nation in the 1940s to, in a generation or so, one of the most ethnically diverse nations anywhere. And they did it all very successfully. There's been hardly any downside to this change in immigration policy. Most of it has gone very smoothly. The people have been assimilated, and everyone realizes that it's made the country a richer and more interesting place. Most people are really proud of that.

Still, you have this great, fundamental paradox: why doesn't this extend to the Aborigines, the indigenous people? Australians are not a racist people. They really do have a sense of fair play. And Aborigines are not hated or treated with contempt. It's more a puzzle: how do we bring them into society? No one has come up with any approaches at all. The gains have been almost entirely marginal.

Yes, there are now some Aborigines who are in public life. There's a politician, a very successful guy named Aiden Ridgeway, a very charismatic man who may well be a prime minister of Australia some day. It's not that they're universally marginalized, but overall...in terms of social policy, the Aborigines are without question Australia's greatest failure. That's hardly a contentious assertion to make. Everyone agrees. The question is, "What do you do about it?" They've tried lots of things. Nothing has worked so far.

Dave: You've written a couple books about the English language and linguistics [*Made in America* and *The Mother Tongue*]. How did you come to write those?

Bryson: I never set out to be a travel writer. I got into it entirely by accident. My first book, *The Lost Continent*, was essentially a kind of memoir. I'd been living in England for a long time, and after my dad died I decided to come home and travel around America, to look at the country and see how it had changed, and how I had changed, in the years that I'd been living away.

Because I was freelancing, I was open to any suggestions or possibilities. I was interested in writing books on all kinds of subjects. An American publisher had seen some articles I had written on English. She asked if I'd be interested in doing a popular history of the English language. This was at the very time I was going freelance, so I jumped at the chance. *A book contract!* As it happened, I was very interested in the subject. I was pleased to get that assignment.

But, for a while, I had these two parallel tracks: travel books, in the broadest sense, and books that were based on library research. The travel books took off, particularly in Britain and throughout the Commonwealth. That isn't at all to say I won't be doing other kinds of books or that I don't want to. I really kind of feel as if I've done some of the travel stuff as much as I can. I'd like to rest it for a while and go off and do something else.

Dave: Last week, I saw a list of the top twenty-five bestselling travel books at another store, and five of your books were included. I was joking with some friends that you're The Beatles of travel writers.

Bryson: That's very gratifying. Particularly in America, it's a very strange genre because it's only in the last few years that it's started to come to life again. You used to get fluky books that would do very well, Paul Theroux's *Great Railway Bazaar* and the occasional Bruce Chatwin book or something like that, but, as a genre, it really hasn't existed in America the way it has in the rest of the world.

I do sense that's changing. My guess is that all of us baby boomers are reaching a point in our lives…we've made our money, the kids are nearly out of the home, finished with college. You get to be fifty, what do you think of doing? Easing off and traveling. I think that may be part of where the growth is coming from.

Dave: Are you working on something now?

Bryson: No, I'm not. Usually at this juncture I would be, but I just finished this damn thing. I printed it out on December 31st. I was terrified that the Y2K bug was going to wipe the whole thing out.

I'd assured the publisher that I'd get them a manuscript by the first week of January because they wanted to get it out very quickly. Usually, you turn in a manuscript and you don't hear from anyone for months. It's only months and months later that anyone approaches you and starts talking about book tours and such, by which time you've completely forgotten about that project and started to move on to the next one. This time, I gave them the manuscript and they started editing it. I had to respond to that, then ten minutes later, it seemed, the proofs were in. Then the schedule for the book tour came along.

I haven't had a chance to think coherently about what I want to do next. I have a couple ideas, but nothing very concrete. In any case, I'm pretty much on the road until Thanksgiving.

Dave: The book has only been out for a week or so. Are you still finding that *A Walk in the Woods* is the book everyone wants to ask you about?

Bryson: Oh, yeah. The one thing I hear all the time is, "I read your book." I suppose that's inevitable. But these days, the market is so tough that if you manage to write one book that more than a handful of people read, you've had more good luck than anybody can ever hope to have. So I don't resent the fact that *A Walk in the Woods* has overshadowed all my other stuff.

At the same time, it's like having five children and one of them is really pretty while the others are all very plain looking. Everyone's always talking about the pretty one. I like the others as well.

Bill Bryson visited Portland on June 15, 2000. Before his appearance at The First Congregational Church, Bryson stopped by the Powells.com Annex. It turns out he has a son applying to graduate school where I went to college, so we talked about that. Also, about a law passed in Quebec in the late eighties forbidding the use of English on storefront signs—you could post French and Chinese, or French and Spanish, or French and Lebanese, but you couldn't post French and English (much less English alone). Bryson's book, *Mother Tongue*, the one about the evolution of the English language in America and around the world, is the one that convinced me he could probably write informatively and with humor about anything. I mean, who ever heard of a linguistics study that keeps you laughing throughout?

Robert Olen Butler
Plays with Voices

◆

A lot of voices.

"The voices, you know, that's the thing I do," he confirmed.

In his Pulitzer Prize-winning collection of stories, *A Good Scent from a Strange Mountain*, Butler delivered first-hand tales from fifteen Vietnamese expatriates living in Louisiana. Outrageous humor and wild imagination came to the forefront in his next collection, *Tabloid Dreams*, a funny yet compassionate investigation of the deeper yearnings behind those sensationalist headlines we find in the supermarket checkout aisle. Now, in *Mr. Spaceman*, Butler brings his talents to the story of a sensitive, impressionable extraterrestrial (named Desi by his Alabama-born and bred wife) studying American society in preparation for the mission his species has been planning for a hundred years.

"Desi is the ultimate alien, literally, the ultimate outsider," Butler explained. "In spite of the surface differences between this book and others I've written, at the heart of it, the Vietnamese and Desi are both outsiders thrust into American culture with a pressing outside need: coming to terms with that."

Call it science fiction or call it literature—the novel incorporates aspects of both—*Mr. Spaceman* is simply the latest product of a gifted American writer whose work continues to surprise and delight.

Dave: How long have you been living in Lake Charles, Louisiana?

Robert Olen Butler: Fifteen years.

Dave: But you're originally from Illinois, right?

Butler: The greater St. Louis area. Really, I feel like a St. Louisan, but I lived in what they call Metro East, just across the river.

Dave: How did you end up in Louisiana?

Butler: It was the availability of a teaching job in a Masters program. Ten years previous to my arrival in Lake Charles, I was the editor-in-chief of a business newspaper in Manhattan. I lived in Long Island, and as a result, every word of my first four published novels was written on a legal pad, by hand, on my lap, on the Long Island Railroad as I commuted back and forth from Sea Cliff to Manhattan.

This was the job that was available, and it was a wonderful happenstance because southern Louisiana has fit into my sensibility very readily, and of course directly gave birth to *A Good Scent from a Strange Mountain*.

Dave: I wondered about that, the influence. *A Good Scent* is equal parts Louisiana and Vietnam.

Butler: I don't know that it would have occurred to me to write about the Vietnamese Diaspora if I hadn't been in southern Louisiana where I happened upon this remarkable, preserved Vietnamese community near New Orleans. Not that it was an act of journalism, far from it. Of the fifteen narrators in *A Good Scent*, not one of them has a real life counterpart.

Southern Louisiana's parallels to South Vietnam, its culture and climate, helped stimulate all of that, but certainly a more direct influence on the book was the year I spent in Vietnam. And the crucial thing about that year was that I spoke fluent Vietnamese from my first day in country—the army had sent me to language school for a year before I went over—so I had a chance to submerge myself in the Vietnamese culture while I was there with the language. I learned enough about the people to see past the surface details, the sociology and anthropology of the culture, to the universal human yearnings that are the real subject matter of art.

Dave: It's interesting that you bring up language right away. Even in *Mr. Spaceman*, which has nothing at all to do with Vietnam, one of Desi's fundamental concerns is language.

Ha Jin was here recently, and because he's so new to English, we talked a lot about language. He said that, as an immigrant, there's really nothing to compare with language, that you can try to assimilate as much as you want into a culture but, as a foreign speaker, you can never truly complete that process.

Butler: And Desi is the ultimate alien, literally, the ultimate outsider. On that point, in spite of the surface differences between this book and others I've written, like *Good Scent*, at the heart of it, the Vietnamese and Desi are both outsiders thrust into American culture with a pressing outside need: coming to terms with that. Language is one of the primary concerns in both cases.

Dave: You use language in *Mr. Spaceman* to great comic effect. Despite his best intentions, sometimes Desi can't help sounding like a parrot of pop culture.

Butler: Well, Desi grew out of a short story from *Tabloid Dreams*, yet that aspect of him wasn't fully formed in the story. The short story was written in Edna Bradshaw's voice [Desi's wife]. As soon as I started to write from Desi's voice in the novel...once, as an artist, you get deep enough into the point of view character, the way of looking at the world emerges.

I winged it more in this book than I've ever done before. I just sat down and Desi declared his existence—the "I am" that begins the novel. And if you take away the period after *I am* and continue into the second sentence, you get "I am The word on the face of the bus," or, "I am the word." Desi is shaped by his words; he's shaped by his language because his species doesn't use words. And also it's the beginning of the religious allegory.

But as soon as he began looking around twentieth century America with the naive eye, as the outsider for whom everything is fresh and everything is meaningful, then advertisements, pop song lyrics, intellectual speech, all of it becomes of equal value. And, indeed, those aspects of popular culture are presented with great intensity. A guy like Desi would be drawn to that.

The clichés that become part of his vocabulary, through his naive and alert mind, they always have a subtext. There's always a spin on them. It's a cumulative thing, the climax being when he says, "Nothin' Says Lovin' Like Somethin' from the Oven," which brings together language, American culture, and theological aspects in one moment.

Dave: You say you were writing off the cuff more than in the past, and yet the book works on many levels. Were those layers fleshed out in revisions or were they conceived the first time through?

Butler: In fact it all happened simultaneously, as weird as that sounds. My work has been tending toward this inextricable mixture of comedy and tragedy, the pop culture and high culture. It's just how I see the world now. It all intimately interconnects. I find it impossible to move through a fictional voice now without all of that happening at once.

Dave: That commingling is impossible to ignore in *Tabloid Dreams*. "Jealous Husband Returns in Form of Parrot" is one of the most heartbreaking stories I've read in a long time, and yet it's ridiculous, too.

Butler: It's funny and heartbreaking at the same moment and for the same reasons. That's how I see the world now.

Dave: What led you to write *Tabloid Dreams*? It's quite a departure from your earlier fiction.

Butler: Late one night in that same Kroger grocery store that Desi visits, actually, I was there shifting a cold bottle of milk from hand to hand, stuck at the back of a line at midnight, and my eyes fell to the rack of tabloids by the checkout counter. I didn't pause at the relatively high class tabloids like *The National Enquirer*; I went all the way down to the bottom of the rack to *The Weekly World News* and *The Sun*. I think the story that night was "Boy Born With Tattoo of Elvis."

I've always watched those headlines. They're engaging. You pick the thing up, though, and the stories are terrible, quoting Albanian scientists and so forth, with no humor at all, no irony. I decided that they were getting the headlines right but the stories wrong, and I had to set the record straight on a dozen matters of importance like "Jealous Husband Returns in Form of Parrot" and "Titanic Victim Speaks Through Waterbed."

I took the headlines and riffed on them. Who's the central character behind this headline, and what is the deeply true and real human yearning that exists at the core of the character? That's where all of my fiction starts, with that fundamental yearning inside each of us.

I actually started scooping *The Weekly World News*. "JFK Secretly Attends Jackie Auction," for example, can be found nowhere but in that book.

Dave: Someone had written us an email asking about "the Sci-Fi writer coming to Powell's on Friday," and it took me a minute to realize they were referring to you. *Mr. Spaceman* certainly shares a lot of elements of science fiction, but really, it's literature that just happens to be about someone from another planet.

For me, what's often interesting is what's *not* said rather than what is. For instance, Desi calls Jesus "a mysterious and important public figure." There's really very little explanation of why the world is as it is or what it will become in the future—which I would expect in a more traditional work of science fiction. What's important here is Desi.

Butler: One of the writing classes at Bard College studied *Mr. Spaceman* before I was there to talk about it. A young man, probably twenty-two years old, shook my hand and ardently thanked me for writing the book. He felt that it was a redeeming, in the public eye, of science fiction, an endorsement of it. He was a deeply engaged science fiction fan, and he recognized this book as science fiction but also, clearly, as a literary work. It was an important thing to him, to take the genre seriously.

The difference between any genre or entertainment writing and art is that the entertainment writer knows before the first word is written what effect it will have on the audience or what ideas or thoughts the audience will take from it. In science fiction, there's a vision of society, a political implication, a sociological implication; they create a work to make a political or philosophical point, and/or they write to produce an effect of escapism, to take the reader away. Either way, there is a preconceived end effect or message, and the object is constructed to achieve it. That is the entertainment writer's process.

The literary artist works from the other end. She does not know, before the work begins, what it is she sees about the world. She has in her unconscious, in her dreamspace, an inchoate sense of order behind the apparent chaos of life, and she must create this object in order to understand what that order is. It's as much an act of exploration as it is an act of expression.

The science fiction elements in *Mr. Spaceman* were logical, compelling, and indeed inevitable because they provided the most complete, articulate way to express my vision of the world. It was not that I sat down in order to provide readers with an escape into something extraterrestrial, nor did I sit down to write an allegory of the modern attitude toward religion, particularly as it has transferred itself with an obsession toward spacemen, which it has. It came out in this other, more organic way.

Dave: Right. *Mr. Spaceman* is as much born of character as anything you're likely to read; the narrator just happens to be from another planet. But, as you say, it's not much different from a book with a Vietnamese narrator.

When Desi taps into the memories of the people he's abducted, for one thing, it just seems like, as a writer, you're having a lot of fun. But in all your stuff, there's so much focus on voice. In *They Whisper*, also, I was caught up in the story immediately because of the voice and the way the narrator plays with other voices. There's the great scene right near the beginning when Ira, who is sixteen, is hiding in a bathroom stall trying to write graffiti in the voice of a girl, trying to find the words and the tone a girl who'd be writing about him would use.

The other voices in *Mr. Spaceman* are so completely different from Desi's and from each other. How did you decide who was on the bus? How did that happen in that process?

Butler: I had a sense of some of the landmark events in twentieth century American history. All those voices in *Mr. Spaceman*, each one of them is from the periphery of a major event, from the first manned flight to the NASA space program, from the Zoot Suit riots to the OJ Simpson trial, from the birth of the atom bomb to the assassination of JFK, and so forth. I wondered if there was a character somewhere on the periphery of those events. That's not a lot of guidance, but I say that only because the rest of the answer gets a little weirdly mystical, I suppose.

The voices, you know, that's the thing I do. There are fifteen different voices in *Good Scent* and twelve in *Tabloid Dreams,* and fifteen more voices in this book. *They Whisper* is full of I don't know how many different women in addition to Ira.

They present themselves to me. I don't know how else to say it. They're different from each other and they're different from me, and they each of them have their own basic yearning, and those yearnings work themselves out in these little epiphanies that surprise me.

A lot of those voices in *Mr. Spaceman*...at the end, there's a little twist, a turn, a beat of revelation. None of them were preconceived. They just happened, and I went, "Oh, wow, that's what that was about!" That's really how it feels to me.

Dave: In your reading, do you find yourself seeking other voices?

Butler: No, the deeper I get into my own unconscious, the less open I am to other voices. If I were not a writer, I would be ravenously reading literary fiction—I certainly went through a long period of that in my life—and I still do read with great pleasure, but much more selectively now. I do try to be as open to new voices as I can, but I don't read nearly as much fiction as I used to. I'm way too busy, and I'm a very slow reader. I don't think you should read fiction faster than would allow you to hear the narrative voice in your head.

Dave: What kind of books do you teach?

Butler: I'm a bit of a heretic in this respect because I tell my writing students to cut back on their reading. Reading is a way out for them. It gives them the illusion of preparing themselves as writers when really they don't have the courage yet to go into their own unconscious. Instead, they retreat into other people's visions.

That's the fundamental mistake almost every young writer makes, trying to write from ideas and influences instead of letting go and getting into that dreamspace. There's a period in a writer's life when you must stop reading as much.

Except for my books. That's always helpful, of course, to read my books!

Dave: Your first novel was rejected by twenty-one publishers, right? When it was finally published, it got some very positive reviews. That's a great example for your students.

Butler: That's right. I didn't sell much for a long time. And before I sold that first novel, I wrote five ghastly novels, about forty dreadful short stories, and twelve truly awful full-length plays, all of which have never seen the light of day and never will.

Dave: *Good Scent* was your first collection of stories, but with the Pulitzer, that was the one that brought you the acclaim. All of a sudden people said, "Oh look, this Robert Olen Butler has been writing great books for however long."

Butler: Twelve years.

Dave: You sat down to write that book as a whole piece, right? The stories were written to be read together.

Butler: I've never just written a story here and a story there and pulled them into a volume. Those stories were all conceived at once and written back to back, as were the ones in *Tabloid Dreams*.

Dave: Do you see yourself continuing to produce stories that way?

Butler: I don't see writing a lot of random stories and pulling them together. *Mr. Spaceman* has fifteen stories in there. It's a novel, but it's a reconciling of the two forms in a certain way. I have a few scattered stories I've written, but mostly they're conceived with an overarching vision.

Dave: I won't mention how the book ends, but when I was about twenty pages from finishing I was across the street talking to someone who asked if I'd finished it. I told her, "I don't know if I want to see what happens to the characters or if I just want to know what the hell he does to tie it up!"

I think whether a reader will be satisfied with the ending is entirely a matter of their own tastes and expectations, but I loved it. I was only ten pages from the end, and I didn't know what you were going to do.

Butler: I think a considerable amount of suspense builds up because of the religious allegory. The expectation for Desi is not very bright. We do not have a very good track record as a species in accepting those who are quite different from us, especially when we sense that they're superior, and even more so when they're gentle and compassionate. I mean, that's how that religious parallel developed. Desi is in some serious peril as we get to the end of the book, but it has an interesting twist to it, I think.

Dave: Are you working on something now?

Butler: I just finished a commissioned short story for *Zoetrope* magazine, Francis Ford Coppola's publication. It turned out real well. It's called "Fair Warning." I think it's going to be in the May issue, as well as the anthology that Harcourt Brace is publishing, *The Best of Zoetrope*. I think I'm going to turn that into a novel. It's in the voice of a female auctioneer in the upscale world of New York auction houses.

Dave: Imagination doesn't seem to be a problem for you.

Butler: I keep pushing the envelope, and I pay a certain price for that. Sometimes people want to pigeonhole you. They want you to do what's familiar to them. That's alright. I understand that's just something one has to accept, but if you look at the record: a book in the voice of a spaceman [*Mr. Spaceman*], previously a Sophoclean tragedy set in Vietnam [*The Deep Green Sea*], before that a book written from the tabloid headlines [*Tabloid Dreams*], before that an intense novel about the nature of human sexuality [*They Whisper*], and before that I was writing in the voices of Vietnamese exiles young and old, men and women [*A Good Scent from a Strange Mountain*]. I just go where my unconscious leads me and wait for whatever it throws up on the shore of my imagination. It always surprises me, too.

Robert Olen Butler met Murgatroid, Powells.com's pet axolotl, on March 3, 2000, prior to his reading at Powell's City of Books. "We have two hundred fifty gallons of tropical fish at home," the author explained after an animated conversation in front of our thirty gallon tank. (The discussion surely will someday find a place in Murgatroid's inevitable tell-all memoir of life in the Internet book-selling industry.) After he talked to our Mexican amphibian, Butler sat down to talk to me.

"I'm really convinced that every fish in the sea has a complex and unique personality," Butler explained. Murgatroid was flattered, of course, when I told him. You might even say he's been preening ever since. "Just you watch," he said, "I'll wind up in one of his stories." Clearly, Butler has the vision and talent to pull it off.

Mary Higgins Clark Reveals: "Pan Am was the airline."

◆

Mary Higgins Clark is the author of twenty bestsellers. Stop for a moment. Consider that. You're thinking, That's twenty more than I have!

Clark also graduated *summa cum laude* from Fordham University at Lincoln Center (with a B.A. in Philosophy) and holds thirteen honorary doctorates. The day we spoke, she'd come to Portland to read from *We'll Meet Again*, the story of a beautiful young wife convicted of manslaughter. Six years later, freed from prison, Molly asserts her innocence again. Perhaps the HMO her murdered husband founded might hold some clues to the truth surrounding his death.

I met the woman also known as "The Queen of Suspense" in the lounge of the Benson Hotel. We sat in big cushy chairs, drinking coffee and talking about the arc of her career, from a young international stewardess to one of the most successful suspense writers in the world.

Dave: A year before *Where Are the Children* was published, you went back to school. Why did you study Philosophy?

Mary Higgins Clark: My daughter, when she was in school, had been a Philosophy major—she's a judge now—and I was always intrigued by what she was studying. And of course Philosophy also covers a lot of Psychology, which is very good for a writer. You have Logic, too, and logic, of course, to a suspense writer, is fascinating. I enjoyed it.

The first course I took was on C.S. Lewis. It was a very good, broadening background. I was always a voracious reader, but I'd gone to secretarial school initially because my father had died and money was tight. I wanted to get a job. I wanted to grow up.

Dave: Then your first published book was a biographical novel based on the life of George Washington, *Aspire to the Heavens.* How did you come to write that?

Clark: I thought he was the biggest bore in the world until I started to do a couple radio scripts—I was doing a patriotic radio series at the time—and I kept coming back to him because I found more and more stuff. Most people don't know he was the best dancer in the colony of Virginia. Do you think of him like that? He rode his horse like an Indian; he was a marvelous rider. He had a very wry, dry sense of humor. But those idiotic allegorical tales, which of course got him free dinners for the rest of his life, he made up all those silly stories that we know.

Well, I was writing and selling short stories, but the short story market had collapsed. I was a young widow. My agent said, "Write a book. I can't sell short stories." So I thought I'd write a book about George Washington. I knew him and I liked him. I considered it a triumph: I'd written a book, and it had been published.

Dave: You were widowed young with five children, and you were still writing. How did you manage that?

Clark: I'd been a flying hostess with Pan Am, which in those days was very glamorous. You had to be between 5'2" and 5'7". You couldn't wear glasses. You had to speak a foreign language. You had to either have college or have worked in PR. And you went through all kinds of personality tests that today would bring harassment suits. You could only weigh so much…when you got a Pan Am job, it was like being a starlet in those days. Pan Am was *the* airline.

It was very glamorous, but I did it for a year and got married. When I got married, I said, "Now I have to learn how to be a professional writer." In the meantime, I'd seen Europe, Africa, and Asia at a time when I would have been a senior in college. I saw a revolution in Syria. In India they had independence, but it still felt like the colonial empire. I was in Africa when it was still the Belgian Congo and the British Gold Coast and French West Africa. Marvelous experiences. But then when I got married, well, in those days you had to quit. I was ready. I'd seen the world, and I wanted to become a professional writer. I had to learn how. And I started taking writing courses at NYU.

I knew I had the talent. When I was fifteen I was picking out clothes that I would wear when I became a successful writer. I was sure I'd make it, but you have to learn the craft, how to tell the story.

For the next nine years I wrote short stories. The first one was rejected for six years. It finally sold for a hundred dollars.

Dave: So how did you end up writing suspense?

Clark: After the George book was published—and remaindered as it came off the press—I said, "Okay, I've written a book that's slithered into a few bookstores. A few people have read it. Now I want to write a book that sells."

One of the tips I give people who want to write is: turn around, look at your shelves, and ask yourself, "What do I like to read?" I looked at mine, and I'd started with Nancy Drew. I remember reading *The Bobbsey Twins* when I was six. Then I went on to Agatha Christie, of course, and Sherlock Holmes. I was always trying to keep up with the author.

Dave: How would you compare the process of sitting down to start a novel back then to starting one now, after having written so many?

Clark: It's a funny thing. *Where Are the Children*, the first one, just was brought out as a classic by Simon & Schuster. *A Stranger is Watching*, my second book, won the Grand Prix in France.

I think I now intuitively understand better why I did some things, but you don't get better and better. You just ask, "Does the story work? As well as another story?" It's like having a baby—the twelfth is not necessarily healthier than the first. It depends on the genetic make-up. Did everything gel?

Dave: Now, in *We'll Meet Again*, you focus on HMOs and the medical industry.

Clark: I like to use something that's in the news. When I wrote *Where Are the Children*, for the first time children were starting to be picked up. It used to be that a kidnapped child was a wealthy child. The average person could let their kids run in the street. *Be home by five and not a minute later.* Today, you're driving your kids everywhere, even in the suburbs—and that was just starting at the time, so I was touching on the disappearance of children; that was what intrigued me.

For *A Stranger is Watching*, it was capital punishment. The third book, *The Cradle Will Fall*, was written when the first test tube baby had been born, and I asked, "What does this mean? What are the social and legal implications? Soon there will be host mothers, surrogate mothers—who is the mother?"

There's so much about HMOs now. I started asking my doctor friends, "What do you think of HMOs? I'm writing a book." One nurse said to me, "We could do the X-rays here, we could do the blood tests, but they don't allow it."

They're sending patients here and there—and why? Because they don't want you to see the doctor. They discourage you from fulfilling your treatment.

Doctors get out of medical school in terrible debt. They're paying off their loans. They have to see fifty patients a week. They have to meet quotas. And they would say to me, "I don't have time to go to the bathroom, and I'm supposed to be a good doctor?" No matter where I went.

So, yes, I try to pull in something each time.

Dave: Which must make it interesting for you. That must keep it fresh. You've been pretty prolific over the last twenty-five years. You have a lot of books.

Clark: Twenty-one.

Dave: And all except the first, the George Washington book, are best-sellers. There aren't many people who can say that.

Clark: I've been blessed. I have many writer friends, and I've seen people who have worked so hard. They get beautifully reviewed. I have one friend, she's in her eighties; she said, "I've written twenty-seven books and not one of them is in print. It's like watching your children die, you know? None of them are around."

Always beautifully reviewed. And nothing happens. So the fact that my books reach a large audience, and they're all out there, I consider myself blessed.

Dave: Do you ever think, I want to do something completely different, off the wall? Not suspense? Who knows what?

Clark: Yes. But I'll always do suspense. I'm always amused by the people who kick over the ladder they climb on. It seems so crazy when you've made a name in something and you're doing pretty well at it, people are enjoying it. Maybe if you're writing penny dreadfuls, fine. The first story

I sent out was for *True Confessions*, when I was sixteen, on the basis that everything they published was so lousy that they'd be sure to take mine.

Dave: That's some business savvy right there.

Clark: But it came back by return mail. They said my people were too upscale. You have to have a truck driver. You can't write about people in advertising.

I'd love to do a freelance novel, a straight novel, and send it in the slush pile and just see. I will do a memoir. So both of those, yes.

Dave: What are you reading?

Clark: I'm eclectic. With me here, I have Michael Korda's book, *Another Life*, which is simply wonderful. He's my editor. Michael is one of the smartest, most rounded men I've ever met. You just laugh out loud. He's a funny, smart man.

I just finished *Charming Billy* by Alice McDermott, which I thought was wonderful. I read *Memoirs of a Geisha* because I hadn't had time before. What else? *Tara Road* by Maeve Binchy. I read a Jeffrey Archer one on the plane yesterday. Also *Are You Somebody* [by Nuala O'Faolain]—which, I just looked at the first bit, but that was very good. That's the last two weeks.

Dave: How do you feel when you see someone reading one of your books?

Clark: I remember once on a plane I was walking down the aisle, and I saw a woman reading one. And she was engrossed! I found my seat and settled down, put my seat belt on, pulled out a book to read. Then just a few minutes later I looked over at the woman and [*pretends to have passed out*]…she was fast asleep! I thought, Oh well, so much for that.

But I get a lot of nice responses. At readings I get daughters and their mothers and sometimes *their* mothers. I don't use explicit sex or violence so I wind up on the reading list for the seventh grade.

It's not that I'm a prude; I've always just preferred the idea of implied violence. The Hitchcock way. How many ways can you shoot people up? I think footsteps…that can be scarier. And I think the sexiest line written this century is, "You'll not shut me out of your bedroom tonight." I swear that's sexier than all this rolling in the hay.

Dave: Are there certain books that you'd like to be remembered for?

Clark: People ask if I have a favorite. That's like asking who was my favorite child. The one I'm working on is the crabby baby that gets all the attention. But when the book is finished and the manuscript is turned in, it's the story I wanted to tell, and I've told it as well as I'm capable of telling it.

Some people will say *Where Are the Children*. Somebody else will say, "Your last one." Someone will say, "The multiple personality one." That's fine because reading is subjective. One story interests you more than another. But I've never turned in a book and wished six months later that I'd taken more time with it. By the time it's in, I've done my best.

It's as though you've given birth to a child, and you never drank, you never smoked, you did all the tests, went to the doctor—you did everything right. And someone says, "Gee, that is one homely kid!" Well, I think it's gorgeous!

Mary Higgins Clark visited Portland on May 13, 1999 to read from and discuss her twenty-first novel, *We'll Meet Again*, at our Beaverton store. She reminded me of my relatives on my mother's side, I don't know why exactly. Something about her struck me as oddly familiar—maybe the oversized dark sunglasses, maybe the rich bank of stories at her immediate disposal. ("What in the world were penny dreadfuls?" I wondered, nodding, in awe yet again at the lack of things I know.)

While we talked, a three year old boy played with two women in the next circle of cushy chairs. A bag leaned against Clark's chair, books poking from its unclasped top. Our coffee cooled to room temperature.

Christopher Paul Curtis
Goes to Powell's—2000

◆

Just a few days before his visit to Powell's, Christopher Paul Curtis learned that his second book, *Bud, Not Buddy*, had been awarded *both* the Newbery Medal, the most prestigious award in children's literature, and the Coretta Scott King Medal, given each year to a black writer for an inspirational and educational contribution to literature.

On the strength of widespread critical acclaim and a large, diverse, popular following, already *Bud, Not Buddy* had outgrown the confines of children's literature to become one of the most talked-about releases of the year. This on the heels of Curtis's debut, *The Watsons Go to Birmingham—1963*, which itself captured both a Newbery Honor and a Coretta Scott King Honor.

Bud Caldwell has composed a list of "Rules and Things for Having a Funner Life and Making a Better Liar Out of Yourself." He knows some things. But shuffling from one foster home to the next, he does not know who his father is. Until…could those old flyers his mother left him hold the answer? Who are Herman E. Calloway and the Dusky Devastators of the Depression, anyway? Is Herman his father? In *Bud, Not Buddy*, ten year old Bud takes to the road to find out.

At Powell's, Curtis enchanted an audience overflowing with children, parents, and curious, appreciative readers. Before his appearance, he sat to talk about his remarkable success, penning back-to-back children's hits after thirteen years employed at the historic Fisher Body plant in

Flint, Michigan. "Writing took my mind off the line. I hated being in the factory," Curtis explained. "When I was writing, I forgot I was there."

Dave: I'd been reading *Bud, Not Buddy* back and forth to and from work on the bus, and on Friday I reached my stop at a crucial point in the story. I realized then how much I was enjoying it.

The books are for kids, but a lot of adults have told me how much they've enjoyed them.

Christopher Paul Curtis: When I write them, I really don't think about writing to kids. I know you're supposed to think of your audience, but when I wrote *The Watsons Go to Birmingham*, I didn't really write it as a children's book. I thought of it as a story, and the narrator happened to be ten years old.

It ended up as a children's book because I didn't know where to send it. Most publishers won't accept unsolicited manuscripts, so I sent it to a literature contest at Delacorte Press just to have a professional editor read it. It didn't win the contest because the narrator, Kenny, was too young for the contest and 1963, the year the story takes place, is considered "Historical Fiction," but they published it anyway.

When I wrote *Bud, Not Buddy*, I just had a story to tell and wanted to tell it. I didn't think of it as a children's book, per se. There are things in *Bud, Not Buddy* that kids won't get, but that doesn't detract from the story. Some things adults won't think are funny, kids will think are hilarious. I don't think that takes away from your enjoyment.

Dave: How long had you been working on *The Watsons* when you submitted it to the contest?

Curtis: A year. My wife, Kay, had more faith in my writing than I did, and she said, "Take a year off work." So I did. I worked on it for that year.

Flint is an unusual city because a lot of the people there are from the South. Whenever they get breaks from the factory, they drive back home. When I'd see them again, they'd say, "I drove twenty-four hours straight," and I always wondered if I could do it.

Kay's sister had moved to Florida, and we decided to drive there. Just like in *The Watsons*, she had a plan, every step of the way, and I thought, No, no, I want to see if I can drive twenty-four hours in a row.

That's how the story got started. It was about a family taking a trip and the year was 1963, but the story was called *The Watsons Go to Florida* at the time. Then I went back and worked on it, but once I got the family to Florida, nothing happened. So I set it aside for a while, until my son brought home a poem by Dudley Randall called "Ballad of Birmingham" about the bombing of the 16th Street Baptist Church. As soon as I heard it, I said, "Ah! The Watsons want to go to *Birmingham!*" and I wrote the rest of the story.

Dave: After you finished high school, you went to work at the factory…

Curtis: Fisher Body, in Flint.

Dave: Had you written before? When did you start?

Curtis: I was always a very good reader and a good writer, but when I was in school there was a different emphasis placed on writing. It wasn't creative writing; it was mostly diagramming sentences, correct grammar, all the structural stuff.

When I was in the factory, I was keeping a journal. Writing took my mind off the line. I hated being in the factory. When I was writing, I forgot I was there.

I'd tried fiction, but I knew it was terrible. When kids say they don't like what they've written, that's what I tell them: "Be patient. Fiction takes a long time." I didn't really feel comfortable with fiction until my late thirties, early forties. I'd tried it, but I wasn't happy with the results.

Dave: And you went to school again, right?

Curtis: The University of Michigan.

Dave: While you were working? What did you study?

Curtis: Yes. Political Science. I realized I was wrong for that when I ran the campaign of a Senator in Flint and Saginaw. I just didn't like politics. It was all about money. The moment he won the election he was fund raising for six years away. It wasn't his fault; you have to be that way. So I didn't like politics. I knew then that it was wrong for me, but I never imagined I'd be writing.

Dave: What kind of stuff are you doing with kids? Do you visit many schools?

Curtis: I do a lot of school visits. On this tour, I meet with groups of kids, and I tell them about my writing process, how I got started. I do a little reading. I tell them if I can do it, they can do it, too.

Dave: Both books are very much fictional tales, but they're entirely rooted in history and real issues, so I can see how in the rush to categorize they might be considered "Historical Fiction."

How did you come upon the story in *Bud*? You mention your grandfathers in the Afterword.

Curtis: Originally, I didn't plan to do a story about my grandfathers or about an orphan. The factory where I worked, Fisher Body, was a very historic place. It's where the sit-down strikes took place in the 1930s; it's where the United Auto Workers Union started. One of my Political

Science instructors at the university talked about it. He'd done studies, conducted interviews with people in the sit-down strikes. I'd never read anything about it before, and he made it really come alive. The workers took over the plant. The National Guard rimmed the plant with tanks, and General Motors said, "Blow them out of there." They didn't do it, but it was a very tense, dramatic time. This was where I worked for thirteen years, and I thought it would be fun to write something about that, something that would be interesting for kids to read, so I did a lot of research on the thirties and the strike.

In the meantime, I went to a family reunion, and they started to talk about my grandfather, Herman E. Curtis, and his band back in the 1930s called The Dusky Devastators of the Depression. I thought it was really interesting, so I took notes.

When I write, I like to have a couple things going at once, and I found that the story about Bud kept growing. I'd write a little about the sit-down strike, but it would seem kind of stale, so I'd jump over here and think about stories about my grandfather.

I don't outline my stories. I don't know where it's going to go. Originally, my grandfather was the ten year old orphan in the story. I don't feel comfortable until I get a narrator, then the narrator starts to talk and I go from there. Well, he turned out to be this ten year old orphan, Bud.

I like *The Watsons* much better, but I think *Bud* is probably a better-written book, in a technical sense. *The Watsons* is more episodic, and I think *Bud* flows better as story. But *The Watsons* will always be special to me because it broke me out of the warehouse I was working in. I'm doing something that I want to do, finally.

Dave: *The Watsons* is more episodic, but there's also much more going on. Whereas *Bud* is focused predominantly on the one character, *The Watsons* is filled with a whole cast of characters, more plot lines. They're different books. That was part of the fun of reading them back to back.

Curtis: In Texas, there was a woman who introduced me to an audience who said the same thing, that the books were very different. I'd hate to be pigeonholed, but I don't think there's any danger of that because I have too much fun when I write. If it doesn't feel fun to me, I know it's not right.

Dave: There's music in both books.

Curtis: I love music. I'm not a musician, but I've got a closet full of albums. There's always music in our house, and it makes me feel good, too, because my daughter is eight and she's being exposed to it.

She listens to Steely Dan and Benny Carter. She's a very good pianist already. She just had her first recital, which turned out to be a contest, though we didn't know it, and she won first place!

Dave: One of my favorite details in *The Watsons* is that the father buys a record player for the car because the family is taking a long drive south from Michigan and he's afraid of starting to like country music.

Curtis: I think that's how you like music—it's whatever you're exposed to. That's one of my fears, really, that all of a sudden I'll be listening to Country & Western. That will be what I like!

Dave: Are you working on something now?

Curtis: The third book is very different. It's back in Flint again, but the narrator is fifteen and the setting is contemporary. His mother owns rental properties and group homes. She's scamming the state and the insurance companies, trying to break this boy into the business, but he'd rather not. He'd rather be a philosopher. It's a completely different kind of story. A male narrator again, but that's about the only similarity.

Dave: Is it any different for you, writing about a child in a contemporary setting?

Curtis: No, not really. Once I get the character, everything seems to be okay. It's a mental trick: you actually feel like there's someone talking to you. I just write down what they say. It's very inefficient. I write reams of stuff that I can never use.

With *The Watsons*, I didn't have to do a lot of research because I was around that age in 1963. With *Bud*, I had the research from the sit-down strike book I'd been working on. In this book, I don't really have to do a lot of research.

Dave: Do you write according to a schedule?

Curtis: I do. I'll work at the library usually from about nine to noon, then the next morning I wake up at five o'clock and I start to edit what I did the day before, try to hammer it down into a story. Writing *The Watsons*, I found that it's better if I just write what comes whether it's going to work at that point in the story or not, then I work on cleaning it up the next day. A lot of things come up that I use later on.

Dave: What kind of stuff do you read? A lot of kids' books?

Curtis: I hadn't read any young adult or children's literature until I found out I was a young adult or children's author. Then I said, "I better read some of this stuff!" I found I really enjoyed some of it. There's some really bad stuff, but there's also some outstanding writing.

My favorite author is Toni Morrison. I like Kurt Vonnegut and Zora Neale Hurston. Then I go on binges when I'll find an author and just read everything. The latest one is Jim Thompson. He's outstanding. Some of his stuff isn't as strong as the rest, but it's like when you're reading Toni Morrison—the language maintains you. Even when Jim Thompson is bad, he's good. He's one of the few people, he and Vonnegut, that can make me break down and laugh.

Dave: Do you have a favorite Vonnegut book?

Curtis: I like his autobiographical stuff. I'm reading *Palm Sunday* again. It's a collection of his speeches and other things. You feel like he's talking to you.

Dave: Do parents ever complain about your books?

Curtis: Well, with *The Watsons*, there's the occasional *hell* and *damn*, and I think *ass* is in there one time—that's upset some people. When I go and talk to kids, you can always tell which one has been prodded by their parents. A hand will come up, and the kid will say, "Why are there swear words in that book?"

I ask, "Are there any words in there you haven't heard? Do you hear those words on the playground?"

And they say, "Yeah."

When you write, you try to tell the truth. You try to make something realistic. But I don't think my writing is going to stir much controversy. You have to get to a certain level, I think, for people to take notice. For instance, *Harry Potter*—witches? I mean, who cares? But I'm not at that level yet. Maybe someday.

Dave: You are developing a track record, though: two books, and they've both won prestigious awards.

Curtis: I get the question a lot, "How are you gonna top this?" But I feel like the pressure's off. I feel like I can do whatever I want to do now. I feel like I'm in a very good position.

Dave: You don't avoid difficult topics in either of the books. I think you handle them with a lot of grace, actually. At the end of each book, you include a note to the reader, and it does seem like you are promoting— I don't know what the correct word is—*peace?* Maybe, if that's not too simple a word.

Curtis: That's a good word. I'll take that.

Dave: Well, it's surprising to find African American role models in young adult fiction, particularly in books that are popular with a cultural cross-section of children. Do you feel like your success has given you more of a political voice in that sense, reaching such a large and diverse audience?

Curtis: I shy away from politics, so not really. I think the best I can do is to write the books. Right now, for me, that's the best thing. I don't want to be a spokesman. What you said about the books being for everybody, that's really the ultimate compliment.

There aren't many African American fiction writers for kids. There's one other man, Walter Dean Myers. He and I are really the only ones writing for this age group. That's terrible. I think it's why the books have been so successful, too: they've fallen into a void.

It was a problem when I was growing up, too. I read a lot of things, but I didn't read books because there weren't books by, for, or about me. I was a good reader, but no books made me say, "This really touches me. I understand this." Hopefully, some kids, African American particularly— but whoever, that's fine—will find something in these books that will touch them.

It's a great compliment what you said, that the books are universal, that you don't have to be African American to relate and enjoy them. I hear from people, they say, "Were you in my closet? That's just like my family." An Asian person or a white person. That makes me feel really good when I hear something like that.

Christopher Paul Curtis visited Powell's City of Books on April 5, 2000 for a special five o'clock reading—his first trip to Powell's. The children in the audience especially appreciated the stories he told about his own kids, including the time Whoopi Goldberg (who recently bought the film rights to *The Watsons* and will star alongside Daman Wayans in the screen adaptation) sat for dinner with his family and gave his daughter an enormous stuffed animal.

Beers with Bryan Di Salvatore

♦

Bryan Di Salvatore's big break came when the mock-heroic piece he wrote about watching the 1985 World Series with his softball team captured the attention of William Shawn (editor of *The New Yorker* at the time), so it's only natural that his focus has returned to baseball. *A Clever Base-Ballist: The Life and Times of John Montgomery Ward* introduces modern readers to the man who more than a hundred years ago organized the first-ever players union. Yes, John Montgomery Ward.

"Owners used the power to fine as an abstraction," Di Salvatore explained. "Anytime you had a bad day, you could be fined for unruly behavior or for drinking the night before. The Louisville owner owed a bunch of money, seven thousand dollars if I remember, so he just started collecting it from his players through fines. A union doesn't spontaneously emerge."

We talked about Ward's impact on and off the field, as well as Curt Flood and others who changed the game. We talked about the ongoing season, too, but to meet Powell's high standards of objective journalism, my irrational support of the Boston Red Sox (and, likewise, my bitter hatred of its rivals) has been edited out.

"Baseball, itself, to the non-fan, is tedious as hell," the author admitted. "My wife is not a baseball fan, and I had her in mind. All those digressions [in the book]: the transoceanic cable, the county fair, the horrible headlines about the treatment of blacks...I'm really proud how the book came out. I've never read a baseball biography quite like this one."

Dave: What struck me most about the book, reading about baseball at the turn of the last century, was that again and again, baseball repeats itself.

Bryan Di Salvatore: Absolutely. There's very little new under the baseball sun. On the broad scale, there's disgruntled players, maladroit owners; there were cries about the plight of small market teams. There were teams back then finishing sixty or seventy games out of first place—it was just as lopsided then as it is now. And there was just as much nostalgia. More than occasional editorials bemoaned the fact that baseball was not the most popular sport: "What's happened to the good old days?"

One big difference is that now teams have long traditions and the league is, basically, stable. Back then—Indianapolis, Hartford, Troy—if a team couldn't make money, they'd close up shop. That's a big difference. The other is that the rules were so plastic.

Dave: I love the bit about moving the mound back five feet to improve offense. They're still doing that stuff today. But when Ward was playing, the rules were changing almost every year. In his rookie season, the book explains, a "batsman" didn't walk until the pitcher had thrown nine balls.

Di Salvatore: Baseball didn't have a predestination to succeed. The idea of a professional sports league...there was no guarantee. It wasn't such a sure success. Soccer, right now, would be a good example of where organized baseball stood.

Dave: The whole concept, not just of baseball having to prove itself, but of a professional league having to prove itself—lots of people thought sports should be left to amateurs.

Di Salvatore: It's clear, though, that amateurism isn't in our nature. It was inevitable. Even back then people were getting paid under the table. It was an hypocrisy. It was about as amateur as college athletics. One guy, Jim Creighton, way back in 1860, was so good he was getting paid. As soon as the promoters started charging admission, the players were going to get some.

So much about the research…it calmed me down. This decade, we're not as bad as we're made out to be. We're okay. I read through files and files of unsolved murders and cases of child abuse, and that's to say nothing of problems with drinking water and sanitation. Human behavior, it was really wretched. I didn't think at age fifty I would start to become an optimist, but in the course of the research I thought, It's nice for once not to have this giant backpack of liberal guilt. Racism, for instance: we're really much better now. We've really made progress.

Dave: I'd read before that Cap Anson was not only a racist, but very expressive about it. And he's in the Hall of Fame. Ty Cobb was hardly a model citizen. Nowadays, well, Ferguson Jenkins finally made it, but he'd been arrested for drug possession, and that kept him out for a while.

Di Salvatore: And Orlando Cepeda.

Dave: Right. Is it simply political correctness? Do people in baseball have no sense of history? Do they have no sense of the people that preceded them?

Di Salvatore: There's a real short memory. And, yes, I really do think we've become very conscious of human foibles, flaws, and in a lot of cases, it's excessive.

There's a quote in the book by Samuel Johnson. He says, "Upon some men, providence has bestowed reason and judgment; upon others the art of playing the violin." God, if you took the same standard they use in

Hall of Fame voting, you'd have to take back about half the Nobel Prizes, the Pulitzer Prizes...

Anson was very popular and had a lot of clout. He was a terrible racist and very public about it, even by nineteenth century standards, but he's in the Hall of Fame.

All that said, if I were king of the baseball world, I'd keep Pete Rose out, and unfortunately, I think, Shoeless Joe. Because as far as the sport is concerned, there's only one sin: to throw a game or to upset that balance.

Dave: You write in the book that back then players were fined for anything: drinking, staying out late, making a bad play...

Di Salvatore: The problem was that owners used the power to fine as an abstraction. Anytime you had a bad day, you could be fined for unruly behavior or for drinking the night before. The Louisville owner owed a bunch of money, seven thousand dollars if I remember, so he just started collecting it from his players through fines. A union doesn't spontaneously emerge.

We have a double standard. We expect these guys to be different from the rest of us. But, for instance, I like to write. It's also my profession and I get paid for it. That doesn't make me love it more. Some days, I don't want to do it. It's like playing in Montreal in late April before they got a roof; there's four thousand people in the stands and you're freezing— it's not fun. But we expect grown-up artists, people who are the best at their profession, to do it for nothing. That's crazy. Architects don't.

It's a curious business. Why do we admire athletes? Whatever the reason, we do. The ones who excel become heroes. John Ward recognized this. He was a star, articulate and trustworthy to his men. He was a leader.

Dave: He seemed to have a better business sense, too. I had no idea that he was the one who first got Florida towns to pay teams to hold spring training on their fields. From today's vantage point, it seems obvious: the towns will bid against each other to acquire teams in order to draw attention to their cities. It's marketing. But to realize that a hundred years ago, Ward was incredibly ahead of his time.

Di Salvatore: It makes incredible sense once it's happened. But, of course, he was well-educated, well-read, and after his playing career, he went on to become a lawyer.

There was something slightly Ripken-esque about him—a little removed. I think you'd be on your toes around him. You couldn't screw up. He was a witty guy, but I don't think he was very goofy. Not really one of the boys.

Dave: How did you figure out how to balance the biographical information of Ward and the evolution of the labor movement he started, then on top of all that, the details of American life going on all around him?

Di Salvatore: The first bunch of research was just about Ward, purely biographical. I remember very distinctly reading a headline, "Horrible Murders in White Chapel." It was about Jack the Ripper. I was up at Dartmouth, doing research, and I laid the piece down and had to walk out of the library. It was a minor epiphany.

Most people will never be as fanatic about baseball as I am. But many of the baseball books I've read occur between the foul lines, and that's very annoying to me. I don't care about old games, you know? There's always another game tomorrow. Reading that White Chapel story, I realized that to say John Ward played baseball in Williamsport meant absolutely nothing. How did he get to Williamsport? And this thing about him going to college at age thirteen…what was that about? So once I puked with nervousness—what more had I taken on here?—I went back, going through the *New York Clipper*, looking at advertisements and realizing that John Ward was playing in the civilized east while the Umatilla Indians were uprising, and Custer...

Baseball, itself, to the non-fan, is tedious as hell. My wife is not a baseball fan, and I had her in mind. All those digressions: the transoceanic cable, the county fair, the horrible headlines about the treatment of blacks...I'm really proud how the book came out. I've never read a baseball biography quite like this one. The Babe Ruth one by Robert Creamer [*Babe: The Legend Comes to Life*] is a wonderful book, beautifully written, but it's straightforward, and I wanted to air it out a bit.

Something I learned from William Shawn at *The New Yorker*, there was always encouragement to follow your nose. To not be the 'A' student and cover the subject with the factual truth, documented, period. It was really cool to keep finding all this stuff. At that point, John Ward had to move over, and I was really glad that he did.

I was trying to serve a curious, smart, general reader. There's plenty of baseball in there, but compared to some books about baseball there's hardly any.

Dave: Was John Ward more important as a player or an historical figure? Statistically speaking, if all you had to go by was his numbers, I don't think you'd be writing a book about him.

Di Salvatore: If he didn't start the union and the rest, no. At most, he'd be discovered once in a while and a few people might argue whether he should have been in the Hall of Fame. Statistically, no.

Dave: Is there a modern day ballplayer you'd compare him to?

Di Salvatore: Well, I think he parallels Curt Flood. Both were unsuccessful; for both, to some extent, it ended their careers, Flood more dramatically so. Flood's stats are not first tier, but I'd want him on my team. Or Dave McNally, maybe, and Andy Messersmith.

But finally, Ward didn't change the game. He was unsuccessful. The Players' League failed. Two years after it was gone, wages were worse than when the League had formed. Babe Ruth changed the game. The guy who decided to change from a dead ball to a live ball changed the game. Messersmith and McNally happened to change the game, profoundly. Walter O'Malley, when he moved. Jackie Robinson—and Branch Rickey, who signed him—changed the game.

Why didn't Ward finish the battle? In all the research, there was a gray space, unanswered. The reserve clause, legally, was hanging by a thread. I kept writing around it and thinking about it until, finally, I came to believe that he was simply fed up and worn out.

Dave: How did you come to this book? How did you become a writer?

Di Salvatore: I grew up in southern California in a working class family. I went to Yale on a scholarship, then to the University of Montana for their M.F.A. program. I wrote for some travel magazines, Sunday newspapers, that kind of thing. Then I was in Guam for a little while, teaching college, and I hooked onto the local paper—just for beer money, really—but I realized I had an affinity for nonfiction.

In 1985, I was working at a supermarket, stocking shelves at midnight, grading papers at the local high school in Missoula, and...just going backwards. My softball team watched the World Series together, Kansas City against St. Louis. We roasted a huge Buffalo hump roast. It was at my house.

I'd broken up with my girlfriend, now my wife; it was just a horrible fall, gray, dismal day. Winter was coming, I didn't have the rent, baseball season was over, and I was standing there doing the dishes...I literally left the damn dishes in the sink and I went down and typed up a little story, a mock-heroic story about our softball team rooting for Kansas City because we'd had a bad year and they were the underdogs. I sent it to Mr. Shawn. And he called and said, "I'd like to run this, and I'd like you to come out to New York and be our guest."

Dave: Had you ever met him at that point?

Di Salvatore: Hell, no! I sent it in the mail! A week later, there I was in New York. A magazine was on the stands with my *Talk of the Town* in it, and there I was meeting John Updike, Ian Frazier, Saul Steinberg (*The New Yorker* illustrator who did that famous map of New York, then the rest of the country in the distance) and Garrison Keillor—because they were showing me around the offices—and my life changed. I wrote lots of *Talks*, a two-part piece about dynamite, a two-part piece about a long-distance truck driver from Missoula, a profile of Merle Haggard, which I'm very fond of.

I think for writers, most writers, it's very important to have someone—beside the person you're married to—believe in you. That's what Mr. Shawn did. And Pantheon, my publisher, with this book. They weren't looking over my shoulder. They were really good.

Dave: What books would you recommend, baseball or otherwise?

Di Salvatore: I'm reading a wonderful book right now, *City of Light* by Lauren Belfer, about Buffalo and the electrification of Niagara Falls. Other people I like very much: Tom Orton has a new book, *The Lost Glass Plates of Wilfred Eng.* I like Tom Drury's *The End of Vandalism.* James Joyce and Faulkner.

As far as baseball books, one of the truly great American novels is called *The Dixie Association* by Donald Hays. I think it is as American a novel as *Huck Finn*—about a pennant race, the Selma Americans versus the Little Rock Reds, a wonderfully comic, energetic novel. *The Southpaw* by Mark Harris. *Blue Ruin* by Brendan Boyd, written from the point of view of the gambler who fixed the 1919 World Series. It's the meanest, bleakest, one of the most poetic books I've ever read.

On the afternoon of his appearance at Powell's City of Books, September 20, 1999, I met Bryan Di Salvatore in his room at downtown Portland's Heathman Hotel. Generally, off-site interviews make me a wee bit nervous (surrendering home field advantage), but the time I shared with Di Salvatore still stands as the most *fun* I've had during an interview. I rode the elevator to his room, knocked on his door, and upon letting me in he immediately offered a beer from his refrigerator. "It's all on the publisher," he urged me, "go ahead."

We sat around for over an hour talking about baseball until eventually he needed to find something for dinner before his reading. There are worse places in Portland to find yourself in need of nourishment. We descended to the Heathman's restaurant off the lobby and continued our conversation while a pennant race played out on the t.v. behind the bar.

Roddy Doyle, Unleashed

◆

Roddy Doyle writes like nobody's business. Each of his titles, from *The Commitments* (Doyle's debut) to *The Woman Who Walked Into Doors*, has earned both critical and popular acclaim. *Paddy Clark Ha Ha Ha*, his funny, pitch-perfect perspective of a Dublin ten year old, won the 1993 Booker Prize.

Now, in *A Star Called Henry*, he's upped the ante tenfold, producing some of the most aggressive prose you're ever likely to read. Henry's father's flight, a mere sixty pages into the book, is one of the great narrative achievements of recent years.

But for all Doyle's narrative acrobatics, his amazing new novel is, more than anything, an enthralling, spilling-over-its-sides story. On page one, Henry Smart introduces himself through the eyes of his pregnant, soon-to-be-mother—right away, Doyle catches us off guard. Compared by some to the expansive fictions of Gabriel Garcia Marquez, *A Star Called Henry* presents the years leading up to and following the 1916 Easter Rebellion in a wickedly crooked, dramatic light perfectly suited to the subject. Henry Smart is a big character, bigger than life.

"I've always tried to make sure that everything that was said and done could, in fact, happen," Doyle explained. "This time around I didn't give a toss."

Dave: I read that the new book is the first of a new trilogy.

Roddy Doyle: Yeah, well, I'm not committed to the idea of a trilogy. I gave it the general name *The Last Roundup* but somewhere or other, maybe on a press release, somebody called it a trilogy. But I don't know if it will be. I'd be happy if it was. When I sat down to write *A Star Called Henry*, I thought I was going to write one book, but it just got longer and longer, and I didn't want the length to become an obsession. I thought, If I divide the story into self-contained pieces, people can appreciate *Star Called Henry* and not have to wait for the next installment, which could be half a decade away.

I wanted the freedom to take Henry's life as far as seems right and as far as seems creatively possible—so it could be three books; it might be four; it might be two. I could be hit by a truck and it could be one.

The first trilogy wasn't a planned trilogy at all. It happened to end up as three books, which then got called *The Barrytown Trilogy*. There's no point in fighting it, but I would have thought a trilogy had to be planned. I don't know. But there's no point touring the world saying, "No, it's not a trilogy. It's just three books."

Dave: There's so much in *A Star Called Henry*. To finish it and realize that Henry's only twenty—it's as if he's lived five lives already.

Doyle: Which is another good reason for breaking it up. No matter how good the writing, I think, you couldn't sustain that pace. You would have had to yawn a bit after a while. *Oh, Jesus, not more adventures of Henry Smart.* I'd have felt that way; presumably, the reader would have felt that way. There'd be just too much to take in.

There are hints that he gets out of Ireland and comes to America, and as he's getting older, in a new place with a new geography, new confrontations, that's a new book. It would be very hard to do that within the covers of the same book.

Dave: Henry alludes to the Utah desert and Chicago. I don't know where you are in terms of writing the next installment...

Doyle: I started it last November.

Dave: So is it set in America?

Doyle: It starts in Chicago.

Dave: What's that like for you, working with an American setting?

Doyle: It's a bit scary. But when you're not working to a strict deadline, that tempers the scariness somehow because the consequences are a long way off. You can do plenty of rewriting and lots of research; you get people to read it and offer any advice that they can.

One thing I found quite liberating—although a little bit disappointing—was I went to Chicago, on the south side, in June, to see if any of the old jazz clubs were still around. I was very keen to see what Henry would have seen as he'd stood outside, under the awnings. But all the jazz clubs that were along State Street, they're all gone; every one of them's gone. There's one that's still standing—it was, originally, The Sunset Café, where Louis Armstrong played—but now it's a hardware store. The Vendome Cinema, where he used to play during the intermissions, is now a parking lot for the local college.

That I found upsetting. But on the other hand it was very liberating because in its absence I can invent. There's nobody to say, "That wasn't there!" Well, I know, but it doesn't matter. I can start inventing.

Dave: I'd assume that most of the historical information in *A Star Called Henry* would be more commonplace to an Irish or British reader than to an American audience.

Doyle: In some ways, I think you'd be quite mistaken. The level of knowledge might be higher—or broader, probably—in Ireland, but not particularly. The War of Independence and its consequences, up until recently, had kind of disappeared off the list of things to talk about. When one delves into Irish history, particularly in the twentieth century, you can't help but have the feeling you're actually reading current affairs. A lot of the posturing and the vocabulary is the exact same. It becomes a bit depressing.

The inheritors of the ideas that were given flesh in 1916, these are the men who planted bombs in restaurants; these are the men who knee-cap teenagers because they won't kowtow to what, to them, is acceptable behavior. That brings an ugliness into it which most people aren't comfortable with in conversation. Outside of academic circles, there hasn't been much about it until just recently when things have happened in the North to shake up that old fundamental hatred. People are now more open to looking at this.

That's one of the reasons why the new book was so warmly received back home in Ireland, I think. The element of storytelling, using real history to tell a story. I think that intrigued a lot of people.

But probably to the average American reader there'd be more that was familiar than to the average British reader, for example.

Dave: When was it published in Ireland?

Doyle: Where am I now? What day is this? The fourth of October? It came out about six or seven weeks ago.

Dave: Has there been any kind of divided reaction from the different parts of Ireland?

Doyle: No, not that I know of, but I've only been home five days in the last five or six weeks, so I feel a bit out of touch. I found an *Irish Times* in the shop just below the hotel and dashed back to the room to read it only to discover it was a week and a half old. Even with the *Irish Times* web site, it's hard to keep in touch.

But when I did my readings in Belfast and Cork and Dublin, there had been a very enthusiastic first response—and the best reviews I've ever gotten, which doesn't measure a book's success, by any means, but it's one thing. A couple of the tabloids had shock horror stories about me mocking the heroes of 1916. But when it came to the events I expected at least one person, not necessarily in Belfast, but maybe in Cork or Dublin, to stand up and give out, but there was no one.

Dave: How do you see your writing having evolved into this book?

Doyle: It's a gradual process. It could never have been a first or a second book. I suppose what I was doing was reacting to the last book, *The Woman Who Walked Into Doors*, which was the most difficult thing I've written. I was a thirty-nine year old woman as I was narrating that book. Every word was a terror—I thought the man in me would take over—anything to do with sex or fantasy.

Even when she was describing her alcoholism. I'm not an alcoholic, but I enjoy a drink, and I can imagine the few steps to needing it. I found that easy enough, but then I had to take into account the gender. As a man, you can be drunk and alone in a pub and nobody will comment on it. There are very few places in Dublin where you'd see a drunk woman by herself. It's a shock. One expects the man to fall over, but not the woman. I thought, Probably the women who are drinking are doing it in private.

This time around I wanted freedom. I was very happy with *Woman Who Walked Into Doors*, but I wanted to make reality wobble a bit this time, to see it through a distorting glass. I wanted impossible things to mix with possible, real and fictional people to shake hands. Not to trivialize it, but I wanted to have fun. I wanted to go over the top. For instance, the descriptions of his physical prowess are way over the top, and deliberately so. Mixing his grandmother in there, learning to read at the moment he was born—in that way it was a departure from what I'd been doing in the past.

I've always been a slave to Realism. I've always tried to make sure that everything that was said and done could, in fact, happen. This time around I didn't give a toss.

Dave: Do you find it ironic at all that the short summaries of this book, the ones that don't get far past its surface, are calling it "Historical Fiction," and yet you're explaining how this was a chance for you to take a step away from Realism?

Doyle: It is ironic and it's not. I can see why it's being called that. We all need labels, convenient words to bandy around. *Historical* isn't a word I can dispute; it's packed with history. It's crammed with angry opinion—opinion that I wouldn't not share with Henry, if that makes grammatical sense.

When I was describing his childhood, I wanted it to be a really roaring race of a read, but also, I wanted to capture the relative poverty of the time, the direness of it, the awfulness of it. To an extent, I wanted to suggest why there was an independence movement in the first place, without saying, "That was why…"

What I find interesting about the reaction to the book is how many people are seeing different books. It's a love story for some people. It's a damning indictment of the modern Irish state for others. A *Bonny and Clyde* on a bike for others. That I like. I suppose because there's so much in there, people can choose what they find most memorable. That's what been the most gratifying.

Dave: That's what I meant when I said it's incredible to realize he's only twenty at the end. For instance, you're only about fifty or sixty pages into the book when his father disappears, but his father is one of the main characters.

Doyle: Because his father is still a memory. Henry imagines him throughout.

The first three books I wrote were fairly linear plots. They meandered a bit, but basically, they started at A and ended at C. Since then, I've become more experimental with plot. There are different ways of bringing characters in, of inserting a piece of information. In *The Woman Who Walked Into Doors*, there are hints of things going wrong at the beginning which are revealed later on, by which time anybody reading with a certain care will know what's going on—so it's not a melodramatic moment when she's hit the first time by her husband.

As an analogy, the difference for me between a good film and a very good film is the quality of the walk-ons. If the same attention is put into the walk-on parts as the major roles, it can be a marvelous film. These guys only have a line or two and they walk away, but you remember them. I tried to do that with everybody in this book. Even though Henry's dad disappears, he's a presence all the time…the mere fact that his leg is there with Henry until the end of the book. Granny Nash, I could have got rid of her quite early on, but she allowed me to give Henry the answers to mysteries that he couldn't possibly have known. It doesn't matter in the context of the book that it's highly unlikely she'd have the answers. How would she? She's in a room all day reading women's fiction! But within the context of the book it's completely believable.

Initially, when I sat down to write the book, I didn't see her going much further than that early wedding scene. But having decided to make her read, I got the notion of having her read virtually everything she could, then gradually the notion of Henry having to rob virtually every book written by a woman in virtually every house in Dublin. The idea of letting her learn to read at the moment of his birth was pure comedy, and boastfulness on his part, and went on to become an important part of the plot.

Dave: At what point did you decide Henry was going to tell his own story?

Doyle: From the very beginning.

Dave: Did it take a while for you to figure out how that was going to happen?

Doyle: I plan as I go along. I don't plan the book and then sit down and write it. I wouldn't be physically capable of doing that, or I wouldn't have the patience. Part of the challenge is to get in there as far as you can and put a certain shape on it. It's a lot of work, a lot of rewriting and very frustrating days. There are times when I don't go forward at all. I'm just trying to make it all knit together.

I don't know where the decision to start off with his parents came from, really. What normally happens is when I start a book I go into it very vaguely. I start off and I get to know the characters a bit. Generally, the first thirty or forty pages that I write end up in the bin because they're not doing anything. They're dull; there's no point.

I think that happened. I began to pare down the nonsense, and I gradually came across this couple. And because this narrator knew more than the average narrator could possibly know, I liked the idea of him almost being present when his parents met. When the book starts, the mother's already a ruin, there on the steps looking up at the stars. I like that kind of storytelling, plunking something there, then doubling back. But it's very hard for me to pinpoint when that became apparent. There's an awful lot of rewriting.

With this book, I stopped at what was now about halfway, after the 1916 rising. I stopped for a couple of months and just put that section of the book into proper shape before I moved on. So I would know at least what I had on my hands.

People ask me how many drafts I do. Some pages it's one. Others it's twenty-seven.

Dave: You've got your "Vote Music" pin on.

Doyle: I was given it on Saturday, yeah.

Dave: This book, *Paddy Clarke*, certainly *The Commitments*…in all your stuff, music plays a prominent role, and yet, other than *The Commitments*, they're not about music at all.

Doyle: In *The Woman Who Walked Into Doors*, music allowed me, without getting boring and pedantic, to put a kind of date on her life. Her first slow dance with her husband is Frankie Valli's "My Eyes Adored You." Immediately, you're back there somewhere in that mush that was the mid-seventies. Also, her favorite musician is Van Morrison. She obviously loves the music. But after she was hit, there was none. She talks about the soundtrack of her life, but there's none for the 1980s. Nothing. She was on the floor, basically, and getting up off the floor.

The music works in different ways, according to each book. It's Country & Western for *Paddy Clarke Ha Ha Ha*. In this book, there are really two things that drag the music into it. One was my decision to use Piano Annie and the piano of the spine, Henry's spine—or any other spine she's working on. She wanted a piano, but she also wanted escape; she wanted out of there. I was very keen to get across the notion that even way back then people were listening to and singing American music. They were listening on their old gramophones to American music, often sung by John McCormack and other Irish singers, but it was essentially American music.

Another reason why there's music was the use of the ballad as propaganda. That's what sucks Henry into the second half of the War of Independence: hearing his name in a song that doesn't exist. They were brilliant propagandists. They would grieve at the death of a friend—like Thomas Ashe, who died while being force-fed. They genuinely grieved, but they'd have the sheet music on the streets within hours of his death. They were brilliant propagandists. So that comes into it, as well. Going back to a time when sheet music was sold on the street. That's how the money was made. I wanted to capture that.

In *The Van*, there isn't that much music, but what's there is escapist. Light pop: The Beach Boys and things like that. What gave me that idea...do you know that film, Michael Moore's documentary, *Roger and Me*? The guy, Rivethead, he's talking about being laid off, how after losing his job he was driving home and The Beach Boys' *Wouldn't It Be Nice* came on the radio. How that song was used in the film, it was a perfect counterpoint. A glorious and fantastic song, then—*bang!*—the reality of a middle-aged, working class life.

Dave: Hearing you talk just a bit about Chicago, I'd imagine that music would play a big role in the next book.

Doyle: To put it mildly, a very important part. It's strange how in *The Commitments* both Joey the Lips and Jimmy Rabbitte tear jazz apart, and here I am now when I'm working at home, listening to it all day, every day. I don't want to give anything away, but essentially, when he hears this music, he feels he's being baptized. He's new. He feels he's gotten away from Ireland. He's gotten away from the misery of it all and he's listening to this glorious celebration.

Dave: As a writer becoming more fascinated by jazz music, does that parallel a movement in your own writing away from anything linear, structurally?

Doyle: No, in fact, these books are generally quite old-fashioned. It messes around, but instead of A-B-C-D it might be A-D-B-C. Essentially, it's going in a straight line. This one isn't as adventurous as either of my previous two books in terms of the plot, I don't think.

Then, you know, there's jazz and there's *jazz*. Louis Armstrong singing *Saint James's Infirmary*—it's the Blues as much as it's jazz. It's the late 1920s. It's not John Coltrane or Charlie Parker, people like that. The people who went to those clubs to dance weren't going there to hear the absence of melody.

Dave: That was years away.

Doyle: It was, thank Christ! Because there'd be lots of empty pages in the book, otherwise. No, I'm not trying to write a jazz novel. I won't even read any.

Dave: What do you read?

Doyle: I don't read enough. I'd love to read more. Time is the enemy, you know? In my free time, it's fiction that I read, usually novels. I have to do a lot of reading for research now, as well. I'm going to be reading a good deal of Charles Bukowski in the next few months because I'm going to do an introduction to a British edition of one of his books.

I'm reading *The Brothers Karamazov* because I haven't read a good, long, nineteenth century classic in a good while, and I thought, seeing as I'm going to be in planes an awful lot the next few weeks, I might as well do it. It's my goal to have it finished by the time I land in London. I just might make it.

I recently finished *Charming Billy* by Alice McDermott, which I thought was wonderful. And *Birds of America* by Lorrie Moore, which was marvelous, as well. I also recently read an old book which is out-of-print called *Chicago* by Studs Terkel. That would be part research and part pleasure because I love his work.

Dave: *A Star Called Henry* is filled with some very violent scenes. *Paddy Clarke* is violent, too, but in a very different way. I'd read it years ago, and rereading it, I felt that it was one of the most subtly achieved powerful endings I've ever read.

Doyle: Thank you.

Dave: It's little things, like when they light Sinbad's mouth on fire. Around sixty pages later you say something in passing about how his lips look. All of a sudden, as a reader, you realize he's still suffering from that.

Page by page, that felt like one of the least linear things I've read.

Doyle: That's the challenge, trying to capture the world of a ten year old kid. If it works, it's because every word he gives us is true, dead and earnest. The violence was easy to achieve in some ways. It was a gradual process, remembering what it was like to be a kid at ten or thereabouts. The freedom, but also the fear. The gang: one would never be a leader, but one had to make sure one was close enough to the leader to avoid being hammered. It came back quite clearly to me.

If I feel guilty at all about things in my life, it's that I used my humor maliciously a lot when I was a kid, in some ways to save myself. I was never a fighter and never going to be. I used to compose silly songs about people, give them nicknames, things like that. When I came around to writing the book, I began to imagine how they must have felt. But you move on, you know? I think it would be ludicrous for me to hunt down a forty year old man with four children to apologize for a rhyme I wrote about him when he was eight; we'd both be equally embarrassed by it.

Gradually, it came back. That book took a year and a half. There wasn't much in the first half of that time. It was very slow. The biggest achievement of that book was putting it all together because it was all sorts of little episodes. I knew there was a shape, but I couldn't find it. It took a long time, putting pages together. I was trying to capture a different kind of link. It wasn't a logical one, not in the adult sense. It was a bit like subtle film editing. I was doing that a lot more than I had in the past, constantly going over things again and again.

I've told people that a good day's work is often a page. That's because I spend a lot of my day going over other pages.

Dave: You can feel that reading it. Because it's not as if you took a bunch of fragments, tossed them in the air, and laid them out into the book randomly. Any particular passage in the book contains bits from three different strains of the novel—which is where I thought it became more effective, more true to the unpredictability of a ten year old's mind, more of a craft.

One of the reasons I liked the ending so much was that you avoided all the easy clichés. You see Patrick's loss in those moments, but looking forward—reading between the lines, what you don't say—there's a lot of hope. It's balanced in a very credible way.

Doyle: I think all the books have that to a certain extent, they show a certain resilience. Part of the human package is loss. We can try to protect our children as much as we can, but that would be the biggest loss of all in some ways; you'd end up with them in the chicken coop, becoming chicken. An essential part of living is that loss, fear and cruelty, confronting it and triumphing over it. It seems like there's a balance that has to be achieved, a certain protection, but letting go at the same time.

He's unleashed into the world just a little bit early. It's no tragedy, though. Parental breakdown, it's sad, but it's so common. Most people survive it quite intact. And other than that, he's just growing up. So the drama had to come from somewhere else.

Dave: Will Miss O'Shea be back [in the next Henry Smart book]?

Doyle: I'm not telling you that. No, I can't tell you that. It would be a mistake for me to say who will and won't be back. Sometimes I have fixed plans and they don't work out. It sways away from the original intention. The book you read is not the one I sat down to write in many ways. That's the same with everything I've done.

Dave: That's why I asked about the trilogies. If you're sitting down with a vision that far ahead…it just seems like such a long way ahead to be thinking.

Doyle: It is. I had a vague idea about the last one. And I know how the second one will end, vaguely. My hope is that when I get to the end of the second one, the third one will begin to take some kind of shape. But if it doesn't, I'm fucked. I'll be *hoping* that a truck hits me!

Prior to his reading here in Portland (on October 4, 1999), I met Roddy Doyle in a conference room of the Hotel Vintage Plaza. He spoke faster and more articulately than anyone I've ever met. I'd stumble around for a minute, trying to phrase a question properly, then when I'd finish, he'd pause for about a half-beat before an answer fell out of his mouth whole, as if prior to our meeting he'd managed to get hold of the transcript.

Sometimes—most times, honestly—writers, in person, show themselves to be surprisingly human; it's evident that their writing is a struggle, however productive and successful they may be. Not so with Doyle. "It's a lot of work," he claimed, "a lot of rewriting and very frustrating days." Still, I couldn't shake the suspicion that he dreams in complete sentences, long looping narratives that inevitably double back to their source at exactly the right moment. I felt honored beyond belief to share the room with him for an hour or so, talking to him about writing.

Helen Fielding Is
Not Bridget Jones

◆

Bridget Jones is not Helen Fielding. Helen Fielding is not Bridget Jones. And yet, talking to Fielding it's easy to understand how a journalist with only one previous novel could have created the biggest literary sensation of the year. She's funny, she's smart, and she's entirely unconsumed by her sudden fame.

Every so often a book comes along that's just plain fun to read. The kind of book that makes jealous writers cringe, muttering to themselves, "I could have written this." Ah, but they didn't—and there's the rub. Sometimes the best inventions are the most obvious. The best books, quite often, read as if they've been waiting for years for the right author to nudge them into existence. And, hey, Fielding's narrator works for a publishing company so there's lots of talk about books in *Bridget Jones's Diary*, and she borrowed the plot from Jane Austen (no word yet on when she'll be giving it back), so there's your highbrow literary connection right there.

Dave: *Bridget Jones* started as a newspaper column, right? How did it evolve into the novel?

Helen Fielding: I'd written a first novel, *Cause Celeb*. It was a satire set in Africa, and I was working on another, a second which was set in the Caribbean. I was a bit short on cash. English newspapers are really keen about novels about women, you know, and they asked me to write a column about myself. I didn't want to do that. But I had been playing with this character whom I was trying to write a sitcom about, so I thought I'd use that character and mess about with it.

I was kind of embarrassed. The *Independent* is sort of left wing; everyone was writing about politics, and I was writing about why you can't find a pair of pantyhose in the morning and losing weight. I thought they'd ditch it after six weeks. Then I started getting all these letters. It became really popular. And it just snowballed from there.

Dave: And at some point someone approached you to make a novel out of it?

Fielding: It wasn't quite like that. It was getting more and more popular, but I was still trying to write this earnest satire about the economic problems of the Caribbean. I'd researched the banana growing situation in St. Vincent! Then I went out with my publisher one night. We were just chatting, and she said, "Why don't you do *Bridget Jones?*" And that was just it.

No one was too interested. I did it quite unselfconsciously, really. It came out in hardback, it got very good reviews, and it was kind of popular. Then it came out in paperback and it just suddenly went to Number One and stayed there for an unnatural amount of time, like six months. People started saying it was a phenomenon. So it's just the weirdest thing that could happen, really.

Dave: *Cause Celeb* and the book you're talking about set in the Caribbean, these books are a lot bigger in scope than *Bridget Jones*. What was it like to write *Bridget Jones*, to be writing in such an abbreviated form?

Fielding: It was really fun. I sweated over that first novel because it was really hard. It's about starving people, and then I was making jokes at the same time. This one was fun, and I was writing every column really quickly. I'd usually try to give myself five hours before the deadline—two was the closest I got, knocking it off in two hours. I'd just do it really quickly, in a panic. Then I decided to use the plot from *Pride and Prejudice* to fit it all together in a shell. Not to say I didn't craft it very carefully, but it was more organic, I guess. An idea which just grew and developed.

Dave: Whenever critics say anything bad about it, they say it's too on the surface. But that overlooks a lot of what's going on underneath, sentence structures and so forth. It's definitely a grown-up, intelligent voice.

Fielding: I've been working for the newspapers for a long time, writing proper pieces. This is me having fun. Writing a book, you wouldn't normally play so much with the words, but I wrote all the *Bridget* columns to word counts. So it was playing. I'd write it, and it would always be over the word limit, then I'd condense it and condense it until it came out exactly the right number of words. Like I'm at the petrol pump—do you call it petrol? no, *gas*, right—and I'm trying to get it to stop at twenty pound.

That had something to do with the truncated style. To get it shorter I'd cut out words—like *I* or *the*. And then make up words.

Dave: Is "fuckwittage" a word in Britain?

Fielding: fuckwitt*age* [*she pronounces it to rhyme with* fromage], it's from the French. That was actually my friend who coined that. She was writing about someone, and she said, "It's just emotional fuckwittage!" A lot of the stuff in the book was donated by friends. A lot of the stories.

Dave: None of it from yourself, though.

Fielding: No, certainly not. One must never write about oneself.

Dave: Bridget says it's different being single in her thirties than it was in her twenties, but her exact age is never mentioned.

Fielding: No. And her height. So you never know how much is obsession and paranoia and how much she's really worried about the size of her bottom.

Dave: And now you're working on the screenplay? Have you written a screenplay before?

Fielding: I started to with *Cause Celeb*. It's different because, in a script, every line has to work. In a book you can get away with murder. You can write around things. And a lot of the dialogue in the book is ridiculous if you actually get them to say it. Like the mother. It's so over the top. And the plot with mum and the Portuguese lover—it's fine in the book, but in the film we're wondering if it will work. If it will just seem like we've gone into sitcom land.

Dave: What makes British humor different?

Fielding: There is a perception in England that our sense of humor is different from America. There was even a letter in *The Evening Standard* saying, "Don't go there, Bridget. They won't get it because they don't understand irony and self-deprecation." But I don't think that's true. People laugh more here at readings. Maybe they just laugh more, but they definitely get it.

One of my favorite lines in the book is where Bridget says to Sharon, who's ranting about feminism, "There's nothing so unattractive to a man as strident feminism." And I just love that line. You just know it's going to annoy certain people, but it's ironic because she doesn't really realize what she's saying. But I know what she's saying and I know what she means. I like all the layers in that sort of joke.

Dave: And is there a sequel coming?

Fielding: I'm working on it.

Dave: It's the same form—a diary?

Fielding: Right, it's a follow-up.

Dave: Is it a challenge to make it new?

Fielding: Well, what's really difficult is the last one I wrote so unselfconsciously that this time…If I'd known how many people were going to read the last one I would never have dared to write it! So now…

But I've given it to some of my mates, and they really like it. They say it's more complicated. I didn't want it to turn into a parody of itself. That was the danger.

Dave: Does it pick up from the end of this one?

Fielding: Exactly. It's what happens when you actually have the guy in your flat—and he never does the shopping, ever.

Dave: I have no idea what you're talking about.

Fielding: I'm sure you don't.

Dave: Do you ever get the urge to stop abbreviating words and write in complete sentences?

Fielding: Well, sometimes I write travelogues for *Condé Nast*, and I wrote a piece for the *Telegraph* about the tour, which was me instead of Bridget. I did one for *Newsweek*, my diary on tour, but that wasn't really complete sentences. I'm not sure if I can do the long sentences anymore.

Dave: Are you worried about going back someday?

Fielding: Yeah, well, punctuation I've just lost completely. I just put little commas and things in to help from stumbling around.

Dave: What do you read?

Fielding: I like modern novels if they're readable. Tom Wolfe, William Boyd—I love his stuff—and Nick Hornby. Like Bridget, I've been trying to read *The Famished Road* by Ben Okri for about six years. And I like Jane Austen. Pat Barker.

Dave: How did you get involved with books originally?

Fielding: I used to read a huge amount when I was a teenager, like four books a week. Then I went to Oxford to study English. But I always did want to write. I got a job at the BBC, and I took it because it seemed too good to miss; then I spent ten years wishing I weren't working in television. Eventually I just started trying to write.

Dave: Is there anything else I absolutely have to ask?

Fielding: You know, I'm being very serious in this interview. I'm talking properly instead of giving you sound bites. Don't you want sound bites?

Dave: Feed me sound bites if you have them. Please! What's your favorite sound bite?

Fielding: Ah…

Dave: It doesn't even have to be about you.

Fielding: Well…coining the word *singleton* to use instead of *spinster*, which has all those horrible connotations. And then the *smug-marrieds*, which is what Bridget and her singleton friends call the married people. They constantly make her feel foolish, asking why she isn't married yet and how her love life is, and she always wants to say to them, "How's your marriage going? Are you still having sex?"

Did I get that right?

[*Pauses. Thinks.*] Self-improvement: So many women feel that they, umm…[*breaks up laughing*]. I can't do it. I can't do it now that I've had a proper conversation.

But it's supposed to be like [*breathes deeply, gathers herself, and puts on her best BBC voice*]: Rushing from the gym to the studio to the board meeting and home to cook dinner for twelve people and the perfect husband and children…'Course when Bridget tries to do that all that happens is she ends up in her underwear with wrecked hair and one foot in a pan of mashed potato. Women like that because instead of stressing out about our imperfections, we can share a laugh at them.

There it is!

The thing about this interviewing gig: As thrilling as meeting and talking to successful authors can be—and it does thrill me, believe it—you never really know how personable the writer might be. Setting aside the various factors that could set any reluctant traveler into a less than sociable frame of mind (a delayed flight, Portland's rain, an upset stomach, a bad night's sleep), the fact remains that few writers have chosen their profession because they're good with people. Just the opposite: writers generally have a lot to say, but they'd prefer to sit alone in a closed room and say it to a keyboard, thank you very much. Which is just one reason why sitting with Fielding was such a pleasure—because none of the standard, socially awkward stereotypes apply. She was a lot of fun, as the fans who came to hear her read will attest. Fielding visited Powell's City of Books on June 3, 1999.

Ian Frazier's Heroes

◆

In *On the Rez*, Ian Frazier invites us to the Pine Ridge Indian Reservation, just a few miles east of the Sioux's original Black Hills land. "I'd done the book about the Great Plains," he told me before his reading, "but I wanted to focus on a more specific part." Toward that end, Frazier immerses us in Pine Ridge's contemporary community—in Wounded Knee, the American Indian Movement, alcoholism, car wrecks, children, and, finally, hope. Along the way, we meet dozens of residents; foremost among them are Frazier's friend, Le War Lance, a nomadic storyteller Frazier has known for twenty years, and SuAnne Big Crow, the fourteen year old girl whose heroic example helped bring long-feuding factions of the reservation together.

A former staff writer at *The New Yorker* and Harvard's *Lampoon*, Frazier is the author of five previous books. We talked about heroes past and present, and about life on and off the rez.

We talked about storytelling, too. "Words are charms," he explained. "You want to know what happened...I want people to know how much they are made by the Native American culture that preceded them and how powerful it is in America. It's like a song you don't even know you know."

Dave: How long were you living in Montana this time?

Ian Frazier: Four years.

Dave: Did you go specifically to write this book?

Frazier: That was one of the reasons. I've also been working for some years on a book about Siberia. My theory on going to Missoula was that it would be easy and interesting to go to Siberia—I could fly to Seattle and, with one change of plane, fly into the Russian Far East—and then it would also be easy to go back east to Pine Ridge. It seemed well-suited for both books, well-situated. And we know people in Missoula. I figured I'd be gone a lot, but my family wouldn't be miserable while I was gone. It wouldn't be like living out in the woods last time we lived in Montana. It's a nice town.

Dave: Missoula must have seemed almost urban compared to Pine Ridge.

Frazier: It wasn't as different as the east. Western towns have a lot in common. People in Missoula, and I think in other western towns, just talk a lot more about Indian issues. They're in the newspaper, questions about land use and sovereignty. It wasn't as far from Pine Ridge as the distance would make it seem. Also, the Flathead Indian Reservation is just north of Missoula, so people there know about the subject.

Dave: William Least Heat-Moon was here recently. That function of westward movement is clear in his new book. He's traveling coast to coast in a boat, and when he starts up the Missouri River, Native American issues suddenly rise to the crest of the story.

Frazier: Most Indians live west of the Mississippi. It's the result of being pushed west, for the most part.

Dave: How did you come to ground the narrative in your friendship with Le War Lance?

Frazier: He and I had known each other for a long time. He'd told me about Pine Ridge, and I'd done the book about the Great Plains, but I wanted to focus on a more specific part. By coincidence, really, he ended up going back to Pine Ridge shortly before I was ready to move.

I had a number of things that I wanted to talk about. I wanted to talk about the question of freedom and the question of heroes. I try to do things according to the circumstances of my life, the way you cook according to what's in season. I try to use what's there. I saw in our friendship a way of talking about bigger questions.

Dave: You go on at length in the book about heroism. Well, yesterday in Portland, a serial rapist escaped from a courtroom just a few minutes after pleading guilty to a series of violent crimes that could put him in jail for more than forty years. He literally just ran out and got away. Later in the day, he was sighted at a train station downtown—apparently, he had a recognizable tattoo on his hand. Basically, three guys watched him, followed him, and wound up chasing him down and tackling him at a station west of the city. They held him until the police arrived.

In the newspaper, the police said, "It's rare to have citizens stop a felon like that—it's not something we recommend—but in this case, we are glad it worked out." And the hero's statement was predictably dismissive, almost verbatim to your description in *On the Rez* of what modern-day American heroes always say: "It's just me. Somebody had to do it."

[Note: The three men have since been showered with praise. Saturday's *Oregonian* [February 26, 2000] reported that some very generous donations from anonymous parties have increased their cash reward to nearly $20,000.]

Frazier: A copy editor at FSG [Farrar, Straus and Giroux] wrote in the margin at that point of the book, "Maybe this is just people being modest," that it makes you even more heroic to be modest.

But I think what is different is that Indians recognized when they did heroic things. The society recognized it, but the individual recognized it, too. There are ledger books, pictographic accounts—autobiographies, really—of some 19th century Native American warriors, and they're just filled with one heroic deed after another. But it's not encouraged now. Just the way the police say, "Well, we don't encourage this sort of reaction." Why not?! So you might get killed, but that's up to you. It's your choice. Maybe if they did encourage people to do it, there'd be less criminals.

And the hero's disclaimer is in every newspaper story. I start reading and try to guess in which paragraph it will come.

Dave: It made me wonder if it's just self-fulfilling. As soon as I picked the story up, I knew it was coming. He probably knew he had to say he wasn't special because that's what the hero has said in every story he's ever read.

Frazier: It's as if the culture is now saying, "Don't be a hero, and if you are, don't admit it."

I once caught a guy breaking into the apartment below mine in New York City. The neighbors had had the radio on, and suddenly it was off. I called them and they didn't answer, which was peculiar. So I walked down the fire escape and all their stuff was stacked out there on the landing, and there were panes of glass missing from their back window. I realized the guy was still inside. I called the police, and they came, and I said, "The guy is in there." The guy hopped over to the next building and ran, so I showed the cop where he was going to come out—there was only one way out, the way he'd run—and the cop caught him. I felt this unbelievable rush. It was incredible. I was so high.

I think if I was that guy you're talking about, I would have said, "I risked my life! I caught a criminal!" It's such an astonishing thing to do.

Dave: I read the section [of *On the Rez*] about SuAnne Big Crow before I met some friends for dinner on Tuesday. In the book, you call her act "one of the coolest and bravest deeds I ever heard of." I had to tell my friends the story. I just had to tell someone. *You're not going to believe what this girl did!*

SuAnne was a very humble person, though. She doesn't fit your description of a traditional, boastful, proud Indian hero.

Frazier: Right. What's funny, though, is that at that level, her legend was created by her tribe.

Native American society places an enormous emphasis on heroism and an enormous emphasis on equality. Those are such strongly conflicting forces that they can tear people apart.

Indian leader, one after the next, did some great thing—then, somehow, he wasn't like everyone else. Yet you were supposed to be like everyone else. I think it created terrible confusion for Crazy Horse, for Red Cloud, and for Spotted Tail, just among the Sioux. How are you this extraordinary person and still a member of the tribe?

And that may also be what you're seeing in "I'm not a hero." For SuAnne, it wasn't like she got to capture one criminal and it was over. She had to be a hero over and over, all the time, and she was just a kid.

Dave: Was there any inclination on your part to make SuAnne more of a focal point of the book? She doesn't appear until fairly late in the story.

Frazier: I think to understand what she did you have to first understand how difficult this life is, the life at Pine Ridge. And secondly, you have to understand Wounded Knee, which was a very important historical force that shaped her and people's perceptions of her.

Her family supported the tribal faction that was heavily involved in tribal government, they supported the tribal chairman, and they were opposed to AIM (the American Indian Movement). But she was also very much beloved by people who'd come from the AIM side of things.

In SuAnne, people found something that they had in common.

I could have made the whole book about SuAnne; I could have made it a book for young adults about SuAnne. But somehow to see the whole weight of what she did, to understand what it meant to do that dance and lead, you had to know all that had come before. I think, in some instinctive way, she really did understand it.

That was the moment in the book where I could have some hope. I felt strongly driven to find something hopeful.

Dave: You quote a Supreme Court ruling about the government taking Black Hills land from the Sioux. The Justice flat out says it was one of the worst things our government has ever done.

> In 1946, the government established the Indian Claims Commission specifically to provide payment for wrongly taken Indian lands, and in 1950 the Sioux filed a claim for the Black Hills with the ICC. After almost twenty-five years of historical research and esoteric legal back-and-forth, the ICC finally ruled that the Sioux were entitled to a payment of $17.5 million plus interest for the taking of the Hills. Further legal maneuvering ensued. In 1980 the Supreme Court affirmed the ruling and awarded the Sioux a total of $106 million. Justice Harry Blackmum, for the majority, wrote: "A more ripe and rank case of dishonorable dealings will never, in all probability, be found in our history" —which was to say officially, and finally, that the Black Hills had been stolen.

> …The eight [Sioux] tribes involved decided unanimously not to accept the money. They said, "The Black Hills are not for sale."

The personal stories here find a context in the research you've done. These people are weighted down by history to a degree which is almost hard to fathom.

Frazier: When you're part of a tribe, a huge part of your identity precedes you. I'm fascinated with history, with the past, and to see what a huge burden it can be—it carries you along like a pebble on a glacier. When Le says, "I'll pay you when I get my Black Hills money," a hundred and twenty-five years of catastrophe is coloring that sentence.

And yet, we can think about giving the Black Hills back.

The arguments against slavery were always bumping up against this: "But it's an institution that's been around forever! What would happen if we got rid of it? How would you pay the people who lost their slaves, their valuable property? How would we harvest? It's not practical. What would we do?" Lincoln's great moment was saying, "I don't care if it's destructive. Slavery is wrong."

You start with, "Is it right or wrong?" Then you act on that judgment. You don't say, "I'm not going to say it's wrong because it would be too impractical to undo." We agree that taking the Black Hills was wrong. Now, what do we do about it? Not just, "We're going to give them some money," because that doesn't take care of it. It's not dealing with the right and wrong of it.

Many reviewers have said, "Well, that's never going to happen." That's very easy to say. I like to think of what's the more difficult thing to say.

If you know what's right and wrong, you proceed from that. But as I say, many people would consider that just mad. But in terms of hope, to say that a wrong can be righted—there's hope there.

Dave: Obviously, you were an outsider at Pine Ridge. Not only are you not from there, but you're not Indian. You were friends with Le, but you talk to a lot of people in the course of writing the book. After a while, was it less of an issue? Was it ever an issue?

Frazier: There was a time when I understood a little better how to talk to people. And I understood that people weren't going to come out right away and tell me everything. It took many visits, many return visits, before they saw that I was serious.

In other kinds of reporting situations, you come in and say, "Here, I have some questions," as we're doing now, and the person will answer them. There, the person would either just not show up or drift away or be involved in something else like changing the baby's diaper—but they would just kind of disregard me.

Some people, the first time, spoke with me. Doni De Cory, for example. Others, I'd been there five or six times, and then we'd just be sitting—with one of SuAnne's sisters, I was sitting on the deck outside the SuAnne Big Crow Center, and she just suddenly talked to me. I'd seen her a bunch before. It was full of exactly what I was trying to get, but if I'd gone in and said, "What was your childhood like?" I don't think it would have come out that way.

Most people were friendly, especially if the subject was SuAnne. They knew, I think, how strongly I felt about her and how much I cared, and they cared, too, so we had something we could talk about. I thank SuAnne, wherever she is, for that. She always provided things to help people cross barriers, and she helped me.

I called Dennis Banks [the co-founder of AIM], and he didn't even say he was Dennis Banks when he picked up the phone. I said, "Well, I want to talk to him about SuAnne." He said, "Oh, okay," and we talked for forty minutes! At the end, I said, "I want to ask a couple questions about Wounded Knee." I know if I'd asked that at the beginning I wouldn't have got an answer; I mean, he wouldn't even admit it was him on the phone! I don't think I ever would have talked to him.

Dave: You wrote *Great Plains* before this, so *On the Rez* is hardly out of left field. But to certain audiences, you're known as a humorist. You've covered a lot of ground.

Reading the opening piece of *Coyote V. Acme*, "The Last Segment," it took a while before I understood exactly what you were doing. I wasn't prepared for it, coming straight from *On the Rez*. It's funny as hell. It's fantastic. Were you writing this type of humor piece while you were working on this book? Do you take breaks, go back and forth?

Frazier: Actually, most of those I wrote while I was writing *Family*. But I don't see such a big difference. The piece you're talking about is about how narrative just carries you along, you just go with it—and that's very much what Le does. He lives for narrative. You're charmed; you want to know what happens, and that's the point: words are charms.

Coyote V. Acme, it's completely theoretical, in a way. There may be a couple essays in there with a genuine first-person, but mostly it's just the words themselves. The author is not the point at all.

But they *are* two different forms, in some ways quite different, and I can't really explain why I do both.

I don't write so many humor pieces. I published a humor collection in 1985. I published another in 1995 or '96. But when I have the desire to do something, it very often comes out like *On the Rez*.

Dave: What kind of stuff have you been reading? Or, maybe I should ask what you've been enjoying.

Frazier: I read a lot of nonfiction. History. And I've been reading Russian authors. Right now I'm reading [Aleksandr] Pushkin, who I think is one of the coolest guys in the world.

Dave: Does this have to do with the Siberia book? Are you working on that now?

Frazier: Yes, I'm hoping to start on that very soon.

Dave: Is it nonfiction also?

Frazier: Yes, nonfiction, and probably travel. Travels in Siberia—that genre is very strong from the nineteenth century and even before. There are all kinds of books about it. I like to write about places, I really do.

Dave: You do a really good job of presenting the oversimplified history of Native Americans and throwing it in the reader's face: *Here it is, the story everyone's been telling you for however many years.*

Frazier: I want people to know how much they are made by the Native American culture that preceded them and how powerful it is in America. It's like a song you don't even know you know.

For my Siberia book, I'll write about these guys from the town of Kotzebue in northern Alaska who went across the Bering Strait on snow machines and drove all over the Chukotski Peninsula to convert Quakers, Eskimo Quakers. This was just a few years ago. They had to get lifted across because the Strait wasn't completely frozen, but they were lifted in by helicopter and they drove two thousand miles in their snow machines in the bleakest, most out-in-the-middle-of-nowhere Siberia, going to these villages and preaching. It's just the most incredible journey.

Well, I have a Russian friend, and I wanted her to see this. The guys had sent me a cassette of their trip, a video they'd made. It's phenomenal. You see these Eskimos getting all geared up, starting the snow machines, packing all their gas and all the stuff they're going to take, a whole sled full of Bibles and all sorts of equipment.

They're firing up their machines outside their houses in Kotzebue, and everything is white; it's the middle of winter. They get the machines idling, and they go back inside to eat breakfast. One of the guys is eating his eggs while, off camera, someone is talking on the phone. The guy looks up at the clock, swallows, and says to the person talking on the phone, "Tell 'em we're gonna leave in…just about twenty minutes," and he goes right back to eating.

My Russian friend looks at that and says, "Real American guys."

Now, of course, that looked just as American as John Wayne. You know, "Thumbs up! Here we go!" It's that moment from a movie: "We're goin', man!" Yet, to me, I was thinking, Look at those Eskimos.

But when she said that, of course, I realized, no, we're all Americans, and it's a different thing to be. What we have in common with native people and with each other is much greater than we think. In the book, *On the Rez*, I wanted to point out what we have that's different, but how below that, we know many of the same things. We have a huge amount in common.

I met Ian Frazier upstairs in the Annex prior to his appearance in the Basil Hallward Gallery at the City of Books on February 17, 2000. Frazier was among the first to greet a crowd in our new, expanded reading space—also, among the first to fill the room to overflowing. Every chair was occupied. Fans clustered on the edges of the seating, in the nooks alongside bookshelves, and around the information desk to hear him read from *On the Rez*.

In the days following the online publication of this interview, we received dozens of letters admonishing me for not revealing the specifics of SuAnne's heroic act. If you've read this far, you may share that frustration. What exactly did SuAnne do that was so special? Well, I didn't tell our online audience, and I'm not going to tell you, either. Ha!

I agree with Frazier on this one. To appreciate SuAnne's story, you have to understand its context. And, hey, that's what the book's for.

William Least Heat-Moon:
Participatory Armchair Rivering

◆

Author of one cult-classic road novel, *Blue Highways,* and one remarkable portrait of a small county in the American Midwest, *PrairyErth,* William Least Heat-Moon stands as one of the most influential travel writers of our time. His latest achievement, *River-Horse,* the third book of a trilogy which has taken him more than twenty years to complete, documents the adventure of a coast to coast journey from Elizabeth, New Jersey to Astoria, Oregon, made entirely over the nation's waterways.

From Newark Bay to the mouth of the Columbia River, *River-Horse* is at once a contemporary update on the American landscape and a throwback to the explorations of past centuries, before planes, trains, and automobiles rendered a traveler's subordination to the whims of climate and topography largely obsolete. It's a modern travel book unlike any you've read before. You float across the country, you drift back in time.

"In everything I write," the author explained, "my primary wish is to make the reader feel that he or she is there. I want readers to feel that they are at my side. If I accomplish that, then I think I have a chance at getting some of the other things across, but if I fail in that, I'll probably fail in everything that really counts."

Dave: We were saying before you came that in some ways your books are completely representative of the people who shop at our store.

Blue Highways has always been one of the first examples we cite when someone asks, "What's a popular Powell's book?"

William Least Heat-Moon: A good portion of my library came from Powell's, a good many things that helped me research this book came from here—a lot of my Northwest section, but other things, too, the Americana pieces and a lot of neat things in the Rare Book Room. I found just one today.

Dave: What did you find?

Heat-Moon: A nineteenth century travel account. That's the main thing I look for. This one is by a Frenchman. I'd never seen it before.

Dave: Clearly, a lot of research went into *River-Horse*, but you're still reading nineteenth century travel accounts.

Heat-Moon: Travel accounts of America, regardless of what century, if I don't have them I buy them. I'm trying to collect a complete bibliography of traveling in this country—an impossible job, but that's the goal. I have twelve hundred books that are just about traveling in America.

Dave: In *River-Horse*, you write about spending four hours at Powell's. A number of people wrote in and said, "Four hours isn't enough!"

Heat-Moon: The first day I try to get about six hours in. Then my back starts getting tired, and I go over to Jake's and eat. I come back the next day—there's always something I couldn't quite get to—and I'm here for another two hours. So it's usually eight hours, which has kept me from seeing more of Portland, but I don't regret that.

Dave: One of the first things that struck me as I was reading was your fascination with naming. A reviewer in the *New York Times Book*

Review, writing about *Blue Highways*, said, "He is a little too taken for my taste with picking a destination simply because it has a funny name." Even your own name, your pen name, is a creation.

Heat-Moon: Some of it is just the sheer love of eccentricism. But some names seem to be capsule histories of what's happened in a place, once you know why the name is there. I comment in *River-Horse* about the Anderson River in Indiana. That's got to be one of the most boring names for a river imaginable. Maybe Mr. or Mrs. Anderson lived there, but the name doesn't convey anything. There's no picture. When you get into a river named Bad River, immediately you wonder why it's called that. In what aspect is it bad? And some names are just plain funny. I think Humptulips, Washington is a humorous name. It's so unassuming, it seems almost self-mocking.

Dave: When I finish a book, I almost always go back and read the beginning again. It wasn't until I reread the beginning of *River-Horse* that I remembered that Pilotus, your co-pilot on the trip, was in reality more than one person. Seven people, actually. But you treat Pilotus as one character. How did you turn seven people into one coherent character without undermining the credibility or authenticity of the story?

Heat-Moon: It was a serious problem for me. When I got off the trip, it stopped me from writing for more than a year. I just couldn't figure out how to present these seven friends of mine honestly, showing what really happened between us and the river, without perhaps risking losing a friendship by offending or embarrassing them. It was a real problem. And I finally decided that I must give them some cover of anonymity. I'll give them one name, a name the reader would immediately know wasn't real.

At first, I tried to make them all male; in reality, Pilotus was six men and one woman. But I decided, No, I don't like that, it's more interesting if Pilotus is like something out of Virginia Woolf—we don't know what gender this person is. That was the hardest thing about it, just trying to avoid pronouns: hims and hers and hes and shes.

To me, it's far more important for the reader to know the truth of what happened with Pilotus than it is for the reader to be able to connect Pilotus with a particular name. They don't know the person anyway, so what difference does it make? But it is important for them to know that Pilotus was afraid, or Pilotus came near to tears. That was the truth I wanted to pursue.

The reader knows right from the beginning that Pilotus is seven people. The first page after the title page says it. Where they shared characteristics, those are the things I shared and presented. Where they were radically different, those are the tales I left off. I tried to make Pilotus a unified character. You found it worked, so I'm glad.

Dave: It reminded me of the feeling I had the first time I read *Lolita*, going back to the beginning and realizing that Nabokov told you everything you needed to know in the opening pages, being so caught up in the machinations of the story that you completely forget.

Your first two books are very much about solitude. *Blue Highways* is people-oriented, meeting people and talking to them, but you're living and traveling in that van alone, whereas in *River-Horse*, you're never really alone for an extended period of time.

Heat-Moon: No, this is my book of companionship, and as you say, I'd never written one like that before. Initially, I even thought about making the trip alone, but I decided it was too much; I couldn't do it alone. I needed help. Then I thought, Why do I have to keep writing books in which I'm the sole traveler? Why can't there be someone else there, especially if that person can change from time to time? That idea became attractive to me.

There are people in *River-Horse*, but the portraits are not as extended, as developed, as they are in my other two books. The portrait that is extended and the characters whom I deal with at length in the book are the rivers, themselves. Yes, I'm personifying rivers, but there's no way you can be on a river for more than a day or so without starting to feel that the river is a living presence.

The Ohio River is a great character. The Missouri, perhaps, is the greatest character of all. It's many characters, actually, as its flow and banks change.

Dave: It's been interesting reading reviews and commentary about the book. It has that strange ability to be popular reading without reducing itself to easily digestible portions. It takes time. What amazes me is how well the book conveys the feeling of the journey. What did you call the short stream-of-consciousness section? Armchair rivering…

Heat-Moon: Participatory armchair rivering.

Dave: Which was fantastic. But you're doing the same thing with more subtlety all along. When I think about what all those lazy miles must have been like, the fact that you've translated them into an interesting story that people would want to keep reading, that's almost the greatest accomplishment of the book. There must have been so much to sift out.

Heat-Moon: It was very tricky. To take the reader to the edge of tedium, which we often were faced with in the slow ascent—I mean, at times, the canoe was making only about a half-mile an hour!—to take them to the edge of boredom so they'll understand that, but not take them so far that they want to stop reading…

In everything I write, my primary wish is to make the reader feel that he or she is there. I want readers to feel that they are at my side. If I accomplish that, then I think I have a chance at getting some of the other things across, but if I fail in that, I'll probably fail in everything that really counts.

So it was important to let the reader know that there are times when you're crossing this country by water when you better be prepared to keep from falling asleep. Given that water's moving underneath you all the time, inattention is the enemy. We couldn't afford to slip off, but it was really hard at times not to. The going would get easy and dull at the same time. That's the perfect equation for trouble.

Dave: It seemed like the nature of the trip changed when you reached the Missouri. The narrative becomes filled with more Native American lore, which is relevant to the land you're passing, and environmental concerns come to the front a bit. Something switches when I read it. Did it feel that way to you?

Heat-Moon: I think two things happened. When we hit the Mississippi, suddenly we were no longer going downhill. There was some upstream voyaging in the eastern part of the country, but it was small. Once we reached the Mississippi, from that point on, we were going uphill, really, all the way to the Continental Divide. And those first two rivers were both in flood. We were really starting to struggle with some fierce water coming against us. Going against a river instead of with it changes the nature of a journey, which, I would hope, would change the nature of the narrative about the journey.

But something else also happens when one gets into the Mississippi—the country becomes wilder. It's much less settled, even today. Not so apparent when you're on the highway, but when you get on those rivers, the Mississippi and the Missouri feel like much wilder waters than the Ohio. The Ohio, first of all, it's not a free-flowing river anymore. In that sense, it's not a river at all; it's a series of dams and pools like the Snake or a good bit of the Columbia. When you go from a dammed pool to a reasonably free-flowing river—*whoa!*

And the farther we went up the Missouri into the Great Plains, especially into the Dakotas, even white civilization begins falling away. The

Indian presence is much more obvious there. We could pull ashore, and if anybody came down to the river, it wasn't the same kind of so-called river culture you'd meet in the east, the people who call themselves "river rats." These were Indians coming down; those are the people who use the river at that point. So we felt very much we were in Indian country once we left Omaha.

Dave: Any amount of driving and preparation you might have done beforehand couldn't have entirely prepared you. How much of the trip was just plain surprising to you as you moved along?

Heat-Moon: Driving along the banks of the Ohio, you have a sense that you know what the river is like, but being on the river is different. The Missouri, which was more than two-fifths of our voyage, you couldn't prepare for it because you can't drive along it except here and there, so it was strange country for us. Of all the rivers, it gave us the most surprises because it was the one I could prepare for least.

I don't think we got hit with anything I didn't think might happen, but some things were more frightening than I thought they'd be. Lake Erie was six hours of hell. We looked out from our hotel window, and it didn't look bad. But once you're on it in a twenty-two-foot boat, it's another world.

Dave: Almost every day, when you wake up, the first thing you think of is the weather, what the skies are doing, the clouds, the condition of the river.

Heat-Moon: All of my co-pilots, when they returned home, all of them conveyed a message to me which was the same. I like to cite one which was in the book: they just had no willingness to deal with pissants and nitwits. The river reduces everything to the basic question, "Are you going to make it or are you not going to make it?" Everything was so fundamental in a way that it isn't when we go about our daily lives off the river. It gave a clear purpose to existence; we just wanted to get through another day. In that way, it was a relief to be finished. But it did make it hard for us to come back; each of us had adjustment problems coming back.

This was an America we had never quite seen before. I'd never seen the country look like this, mile after mile. Emotionally, it's a different place to spend so many hours each day, bobbing on water. Even if you do see shorelines, it's not a land voyage, and you're very much aware of that.

Dave: Did the trip change your opinions? What did you learn?

Heat-Moon: I came away much more optimistic than I was before I left, in part because the country looks better from the rivers than it does from our highways. It's far less junky, fewer billboards and so forth. And I also came away feeling that when we dedicate ourselves to trying to make improvements—in any environmental situation, but in this case, in our waters—we can do it. The Clean Water Act of the 1970s has made tremendous improvements upon our waterways. The East River is not an unpleasant place to be anymore. The Ohio has big problems with litter, but even it, for the most part, was a beautiful waterway. Then places like the Salmon River...we just felt that was virtually pristine water; we were drinking from springs up above on the hillsides, drinking straight from the hillsides.

A lot of that is the gift of people working and trying to implement The Clean Water Act, lots of individual actions. I came away feeling that if we turn our minds to something, we really can make a difference. I don't think, beforehand, I was feeling quite so good about that.

Dave: I hadn't read *PrairyErth* until recently. I was surprised how funny it is. The scene where you're sitting in the van, hiding in there for twelve hours with a box of Fig Newtons, a deep supply of coffee, and a pencil, just watching what happens outside—and virtually *nothing* happens, of course, because you're in Cedar Point, Kansas. That whole experience must have been completely different, writing a book that was so focused, grounded in one place, rather than documenting a trip.

Heat-Moon: I think the two books are just about as different as one writer could produce, given that I'm working in the same format—that is, nonfiction, and specifically, travel. I do think *PrairyErth* is a travel book, albeit in a small place. Otherwise, other than maybe stylistic considerations and concerns I address, they seem like books by two different people, or certainly a person attempting to do two different things.

I think most travel writers are attempting to penetrate the landscape. *PrairyErth* is an attempt, almost literally, to get inside the land, itself. There's that one scene in there in which I tried to look down a gas well that was so deep it went down to rocks that were a billion years old. I wanted to see, in a sense, the basement of that prairie. In this story, the depth is of another sort; I'm trying to probe into the depth, or the nature, of rivers. They're very different books.

Dave: Was that a conscious decision? How far along were you in your conception of *River-Horse* as you were finishing *PrairyErth*?

Heat-Moon: When I finished the actual writing, it wasn't there at all, although the ideas for all three of my books came about, the seed for them, at least, together—I think it was in 1974. They all came about from studying road maps, trying to see what things I could learn. As I say in that book, I read maps maybe the way some people do holy writ: I read it again and again, the same map, looking for new discoveries, and I'm always surprised that every time I look there's something there I hadn't noticed before or I see it in a different way. The three books came out of that same Rand McNally road atlas. Best book purchase I ever made, I guess.

Dave: In *River-Horse*, then also in the Afterword to the new edition of *Blue Highways*, you mention working on a novel.

Heat-Moon: Well, I haven't begun anything yet. I'm not sure that I'm going to turn to fiction, but I think there's a good chance I might. I need to make a change at this point; I need to do something a little different. How different it's going to be from the kind of nonfiction that I write, I don't know, but it seems to me it's not going to be as big a change as some people think.

Like so many people in the New Journalism, I'm using techniques I learned from fiction writers: plot, character, certainly setting galore. Those things will be similar; it's just that certain other issues will become more prominent. The big thing will be not having the plot already laid out for me simply because it's what happened; the big thing will be using the imagination to find the plot that *might* happen. In terms of writing character and setting, I think it will be a continuation of what I'm doing now. But I must say, it's enough of a difference that I'm a little intimidated by it.

Dave: I'd imagine you were intimidated by *River-Horse* before you began.

Heat-Moon: I was intimidated by the voyage, yes. I'd wanted to make a trip like that since 1991. I sold the idea for the book to Houghton Mifflin when I was in Seattle on the book tour for *PrairyErth*. I said I'd do a nonfiction book about water. One of the possibilities was to make a journey, or several journeys, on water. The one I really wanted to do was coast to coast, but I thought I couldn't do it, it was too hard. It took about three and a half years to make up my mind that that was the one I had to do to get at some of these issues I wanted to talk about. It was the most intimidating undertaking I've ever made.

Dave: How long did it take you to write the book after the trip was finished?

Heat-Moon: I wrote the first draft of this book faster than either of the other two. It took just about two years to do it. The others took about four. But what that meant was I re-wrote *River-Horse* ten times; I re-wrote the others just eight.

Dave: I thought it was great that you included some of the original log-book entries. They provide context; a reader can see where the narrative started. You talk about someday writing fiction. Everything from turning Pilotus into one consistent character to the way you present the boat— the boat, *Nikawa*, is as big a character as anyone or anything in the story—that, in itself, is storytelling; that's novelization.

Who are the fiction writers you admire?

Heat-Moon: In terms of being influenced for a good number of years, William Faulkner and James Agee. I went through a Hemingway period, but that didn't last very long. I was quite young.

But in terms of influencing *River-Horse*, I felt much closer to nineteenth century river travelers. I've even attempted to give more of a nineteenth century cast to the style of the book because that was a time when we, as Americans, were really in touch with our waterways. It was the great American river century, at least in white terms. So I thought that seemed appropriate.

Also, the form of the book is a logbook—the subtitle is *The Logbook of a Boat Across America*—so I tried to build the form of the book around that of nineteenth century river travel.

Dave: The book seems more environmentally conscious than your past work. Maybe not more than *PrairyErth*, but in a different way. Maybe just more up front.

Heat-Moon: Issue-oriented, yes, and more clear on my positions. Particularly on issues that affect the west: The Grazing Act, The Mining Act, The Clean Water Act, though that one affects us all. And as you know, the book has, at the end, a section called "If You Want To Help." I picked out six groups that deal with issues that come up in *River-Horse* with the idea that if somebody wants to go beyond just reading about these issues, if somebody wants to do something, here are some addresses and phone numbers. In that way, I wanted *River-Horse* to be a kind of service book to help along some of these environmental causes that have so much to do with the quality of life we're going to face in the next century.

William Least Heat-Moon visited Powell's City of Books on November 16, 1999. The conversation presented here took place before his reading and book signing. Afterwards, when the overflow audience had dispersed, Bill joined a group of us for pitchers of beer at the Bridgeport Brewery here on Portland's west side. I never did get around to telling him that years ago I wandered around the country for ten weeks in a van with a dog-eared copy of *Blue Highways* in the back seat.

A.M. Homes Is a Big Fat Liar

◆

"A Real Doll," A.M. Homes's short story about a boy who dates, seduces, and eventually rapes his sister's Barbie doll, is one of the most twisted, disturbing pieces of fiction I've ever read—and also one of the best. It's shocking, funny, strange, challenging, and indescribably real.

Homes's longer work, including her new novel, *Music for Torching*, shares many of those same qualities. When I heard the premise of the new book I knew I wanted to read it: fed up with their suburban lives, an arguing couple decides against barbecuing dinner and instead uses the lighter fluid to set their house on fire. As the house burns, they take their young children out for steak and ice cream. And that's just the first twenty pages. These are mixed up people she's writing about. Drugged, confused children in middle aged bodies. Unsettlingly recognizable. In her writing we find moments of clarity in the least suspected places.

"I think I can't help but write something sort of serious, that's my inclination," she said, "but I also wanted people to laugh along with it. *Oh my God, I understand these people.* It's funny and it's awful. And they keep reading."

Homes teaches at Columbia. She likes Roald Dahl and Don Delillo. She's very funny. Before her reading at Powell's, we talked about her novels and stories and their place within the context of American surrealist fiction. And other things, too, like summer rental houses that are sticky to touch.

Dave: *Music for Torching* started as a short story, right?

A. M. Homes: It started twice as a short story—originally, as "Adults Alone," from *The Safety of Objects*, with Elaine and Paul. Then I really didn't think about them for a long time—until "Music for Torching," the short story.

I'd rented a house that was sticky. It was actually tacky to touch it. I was so upset that I had to leave. There went my summer. I was so depressed. I tried to turn it in for a non-sticky house, but the real estate agent kind of screwed me over. So I went home, and I wrote this story. It was, oddly, to impress someone, too, to get someone's attention a bit. I jokingly said, "Oh, here's a short story. It's my *New Yorker* story." Swagger, swagger. My fingers were completely crossed in prayer. I think I wrote it that summer, which was probably the summer before *End of Alice* came out, and *The New Yorker* printed it in the fall, if I remember correctly.

Dave: Did you put the story away for a while before it became a novel?

Homes: No. I was just working. I had absolutely no intention of turning it into a novel. I actually don't approve of stories turning into novels; I'm completely opposed to it.

But I'd finished the story; no one had bought it yet, and I was still sort of writing. I thought, That's fine, it's just a little phlegm, a clearing of the throat. And all of a sudden I had about sixty pages. So now it was, Oh, this is a little annoying. Is it a novella? What are we talking about here?—they burn down their house on page fifteen. At about a hundred, a hundred and thirty pages, I had to start paying attention. Somebody has to be driving the car. If it was going to be a novel, I had to start thinking about how it was going to sustain itself considering what happens in the beginning. But I still am morally opposed to turning stories into novels.

Dave: When did you get over that?

Homes: I'm still not. *The End of Alice* had knocked the wind out of me in a lot of ways, just writing it. I think *Music for Torching* happened in part because there was no other large thing looming. I was finally like, Oh alright, you can be the next novel if you want to. But again, very grudgingly.

Dave: I mentioned *Alice* in Powell's online discussion group, and more people had read it than I ever would have guessed, yet everyone was talking about how it made them so uncomfortable that they sold the book immediately after finishing it. As if they were scared to have it on their shelves or something.

Homes: A lot of people have read that book, and I'm more frightened of the ones that tell me, "Oh, I really love that book *End of Alice*, yeah." I just want to say, "What are you thinking?"

Dave: Well, you wrote it.

Homes: I know. But it's a profoundly disturbing book. It's a serious book, an upsetting book. And a thought provoking book, I hope. Those are the best case scenarios. A lot of people thought they somehow had bonded with me on their most secret, twisted perversions, and they hadn't.

That book meant a lot to me. Intellectually and artistically, it was the hardest thing I've ever done. Writing fiction, to me, means being inside other people's heads. But this head was so completely unfamiliar and dark. And his language was a language that I didn't speak. I had to learn a new vocabulary. No joking. I was literally out buying Latin dictionaries, studying up.

He's also odd because he's smart, but not as smart as he thinks he is. The more he remembers about what he actually did, the crazier he goes. They show him a picture of a dead girl and he sees flowers. By the end, he's completely unraveled.

It was hard to create someone who in the course of a book comes so completely undone—because I was also relying on him to tell the story. It was like drunk driving, or driving under the influence of something.

Dave: What was it like to write that, emotionally?

Homes: It was really, really hard. I remember feeling awful by the end of it. I was depressed and sad. I went into a bookstore to do some research, looking up stabbings and forensic reports, the details of these sorts of things, and I remember standing in the bookstore, literally crying.

I once jokingly told someone that every book is like a relationship. They're four or five years long—that's not so bad. They're serious. They demand a lot of attention. But I remember thinking that I wanted to have one with someone who's not so crazy and peculiar and demanding.

So I started dating Paul and Elaine. I wanted to write something that was funnier. *Alice* has a lot humor in it, but it's buried in there. And I wanted to write about marriage and family. I think I can't help but write something sort of serious, that's my inclination, but I also wanted people to laugh along with it. *Oh my God, I understand these people.* It's funny and it's awful. And they keep reading.

Dave: That describes it well. *Music For Torching* is disturbing, but in a completely different way than *End of Alice.* It's a lot more entertaining. It's more fun to read.

Homes: With *Alice*, I wanted to write a book where people, at times, would be very drawn into it, seduced by it—and on the very next page want to throw the book across the room because they're so upset that they've been seduced, that they've been had by this guy. Then a minute or two passes and they have to get up and go get it so they can pick it up and read some more.

I like that book a lot. I feel, as a writer, that I worked incredibly hard and I did what I wanted to do. A big thing was to not shy away from the material. My responsibility is to not worry about what people are going to think, but to worry about the character and how to most accurately represent him.

Dave: It seemed to me the most technically impressive of your stuff. Underneath the story, I found myself thinking, I can't really believe she's pulling this off, the narrator telling the girl's story and all the ways that's refracting.

Homes: It's like a kaleidoscope. You think, What's real here? That's also why Alice's letters are in there: for grounding. And the reality is that she's probably much less interesting than he makes her out to be.

Dave: Reading "A Real Doll" [from Homes's short story collection, *The Safety of Objects*], I got the same feeling. Technically, the story was so impressive. For instance, right at the start, the first two lines are present tense; the rest of the story is past. It's almost as if the story falls, whole, out of that shell.

To chronicle a relationship between a boy and a Barbie doll without undermining the seriousness of it—that not only requires an incredible attention to craft but also a remarkable subtlety because, for the story to work, the reader has to accept the premise entirely from the start. And the narrator completely pulls it off.

Homes: I was able to do in that story what I feel I did in *Alice*—the real and the surreal simultaneously existing, neither dominating the other. It was hard to do in a story and harder, really, in a novel, but for me those two have the same platform. *Music For Torching* and *In a Country of Mothers* are fairly linear and normal—I don't know if I should use that word, but they're more straightforward. They exist within a very specific time frame.

Dave: *Jack*, also. You were younger, obviously, but the tone of that book is so much different, so much warmer.

Homes: I wrote that book as an undergraduate, when I was nineteen, as part of a homework assignment. Now it's in something like its eleventh paperback printing and it's sold all over the world. Sometimes I wish I could write that way again—that *well* again. I think there's a clarity to it and a purity that there's no way I have now. I know too much. The clunkiness with which that book was written, I still remember. It amazes me that I could speak at that age, much less write a book. It's a very sweet book. It's a nice story.

Dave: Exactly—it's a nice book. And you wrote *The End of Alice!*

Homes: I know, exactly. *Alice* got cancelled in France, cancelled in Switzerland, and banned in parts of England. *Jack* actually won the highest German literature prize. In Belgium, *Jack* is on school reading lists.

Dave: David Leavitt said of *The Safety of Objects*—but I think it applies to *Alice* and *Music*, too—"The more bizarre things get, the more impressed one is by A.M. Homes's skill as a realist." I read that quote, and I thought, Yes, exactly. What do you think?

Homes: Life is incredibly surrealistic. Especially where I live, in New York City, the weirdest things happen every day. So many things are so odd. You just have to be aware of it. Also, it's just part of the American surrealist tradition. I think of John Cheever and stories like "The Swimmer." The character swims across Westchester County, but it's told so realistically that you don't even notice it.

I love that stuff. Delillo does it too. The Airborne Toxic Event in *White Noise*—you go, "Yeah, sure." Then it happens in real life five minutes later. It's like *Close Encounters*, the odd mix of the surreal and the real. Richard Dreyfuss is out there in suburbia playing with his mashed potatoes.

Dave: Is this the kind of stuff you read?

Homes: I read student homework.

Dave: At Columbia?

Homes: Right.

Dave: What's important to you, as a writer, to teach young writers?

Homes: You can talk to people about how they should structure their sentences or how information should unfold, but I think, in writing classes, one of the big things that people don't talk about enough is content. If you want people to come to your story, there has to be a reason. Whether it's the pedophile telling his story in *The End of Alice* or Paul and Elaine burning down their house in *Music for Torching*, something has to be going on. It's almost like the question from the Jewish holidays, "Why is this night different from any other night?"

Dave: Your characters do act. For instance, when Paul gets the tattoo, he seems to experience practically no transitional thought.

Homes: Right. But the funny thing is that they're always in their heads. They're always obsessively thinking. Elaine is thinking about the house: *What should we do about the house?* Paul thinks about thinking: *How fast do people think? Is thinking faster than worrying?*

They're not all that aware of consequences. Although he thinks, *If I have an affair and I spend the money, Elaine might find out.* Not, *It's a bad thing.* To Paul, it's more of a cash problem than a moral issue.

Dave: Maybe it feels like there's so much action because the third person voice that's telling the story isn't very intrusive at all. The events just keep rolling by. Until, there's a point near the end of the novel where the narrator interrupts to make a statement about people and how they live, about loneliness, and the interruption jumps out at the reader because it hasn't been happening for three hundred pages.

Homes: There's a few of those little ones. Somebody tried to get me to take them out, but I thought, No, I like them, I'm leaving them in. It's true: the narrative, despite being third-person, belongs alternately to Paul and Elaine, and it's told from a peculiar distance that isn't much distance at all.

Dave: What authors do you use in class?

Homes: It depends a lot on the class and who's in there. I use a lot of the old stand-bys: Carver, Cheever...I use Michael Cunningham's story, "White Angel," that was part of *Home at the End of the World*. I use a little bit of Grace Paley. Then I have my personal favorites. Russell Edson writes these wacky, I don't know, something like prose poems. Richard Yates wrote *Revolutionary Road* in 1971, which I really see as a predecessor to *Music for Torching*. It's one of the first books that took apart suburbia. I like his short stories a lot, too.

When you're teaching undergraduates, you find they're often writing about childhood, and one of the challenges is how you get them to do that without writing *for* children.

Dave: Do you read much children's literature? That's one area where the real often bleeds into the surreal.

Homes: Sometimes. Stuff like Chris Van Allsburg. *Jumanji*, I love, which is totally wacko. *The Little Prince*—I love that story. Roald Dahl—is it *Solo*, the autobiographical story when he was in the R.A.F.?—he was flying his plane through Africa and he decapitated a giraffe. The image is so cool: the giraffe's neck and the blood on the wing of the plane.

Dave: I once read an interview you did with Grace Paley. I found a copy of it this morning. How did you come about doing that?

Homes: She was my teacher. At Sarah Lawrence, when I was little. Grace taught me a lot.

Dave: Your writing is so different, yet obviously you have an immense amount of respect for her.

Homes: Absolutely. But I think what she taught me most was the notion of writing the truth according to the character. People always talk about, "How can you write about marriage? How can you write about a boy dating a Barbie doll? You're none of these things."

That's because I'm a fiction writer. I'm a big, fat liar.

Grace really talked about figuring out what's accurate for the people you're writing about, not what's accurate for you. You can write what you know for about an hour and a half—then it's over.

I interviewed A.M. Homes prior to her appearance at Powell's City of Books on May 24, 1999. Two other women sat in the room as we talked, which I found a bit awkward at first. It wasn't a very big room. It felt a little like the time in third grade when I went to Baskin Robbins with Angie Bascomb and her aunts. Until we started talking, then it was fine.

After her reading, Homes and I wandered through the City— Green Room, Blue Room, Gold, and Rare—asking various staff members for advice, collecting reading material for the rest of her book tour, young adult fiction and fantasy, mostly, good reading for the planes.

Pico Iyer's Mongrel Soul

◆

"Suddenly, the flames were curling seventy feet above my living room," *The Global Soul* begins. The author's house burns down, and next thing we know we're caroming from island to city to jungle, culture-hopping the globe, dizzy in the blur of it all.

Born to Indian parents, raised back and forth between England and the United States, and living now in Japan when he's not visiting some far-flung corner of the earth, Pico Iyer calls himself "a mongrel," part of a fast-growing population of global souls who exist in many cultures all at once "and so fall in the cracks between them."

A worldwide television network forbids the use of the word *foreign* on its broadcasts; Olympic athletes offer their bodies to distant nations in order to improve their medal hopes; various bestselling authors sell the majority of their books in translation; an international burger chain gains a foothold in Asia while, suddenly, a half dozen Thai restaurants appear in your city; and meanwhile, here you are, surfing the Net…

"All of us," Iyer said, "whether we move or not, are having to deal with this crossing of cultures."

Day after day, an ever-increasing traffic of humanity skips from continent to continent, hemisphere to hemisphere, the citizens of a community beyond nations, and for more and more people, the notion of home has little to do with any particular part of the planet. If this isn't quite what we'd imagined home would be, well, home has never been quite like this before.

Dave: We have at least one thing in common. In your Acknowledgments, I noticed you mentioned "the craggy transports of Van Morrison."

Pico Iyer: Really? You're a huge fan?

Dave: Along the same lines as you, I'm guessing.

Iyer: Have you seen a book called *The Spiritual Tourist*? It's by an English rock and roll journalist called Mick Brown. He goes around to the major teachers in the world, the Dalai Lama, Sai Baba in India, southern Baptists in Tennessee, but he begins the book with Van Morrison. He brings you into Van's inner sanctuary. It's very touching if you're a fan because it shows you why he maintains that gruff, even hostile exterior, what he's protecting.

But I love the fact, apart from anything, that in the context of this global world and the inundation of data, Van Morrison is so much going his own way, completely indifferent to distraction and the moment. He's the great modern mystic, as well as a soulful singer.

Dave: I hadn't had a chance to read your work until recently, but I really enjoyed *The Global Soul*. I found, especially toward the end, that a real shape emerged from the narrative. The last chapter felt very much earned.

Iyer: I begin deliberately with those dizzying surfaces and passageways—movement, an inundation of data, which I think reflects how the world is today—and you have to fight your way through it to get to the stillness and the settledness and the space that begins to open up in those last two chapters. The first chapters make you almost jet-lagged; there's so much information that you can't tell right from left, east from west.

In part, the book is about the passage from speed to slowness and surface to depth. To me, that's the big challenge in the global era. The need for stillness, for seceding from that world, is greater than ever.

Dave: You mention near the beginning that attention skills fall five hundred percent after a long distance flight. It seems like you're always getting off a plane. How do you get anything done?

Iyer: I'm working hard to travel less because it *is* very difficult to travel and write at the same time.

In the past, I've visited remote places—North Korea, Ethiopia, Easter Island—partly as a way to visit remote states of mind, remote parts of myself that I wouldn't ordinarily explore. One reason I dwell on jet lag in this book is because it's a different state of being, one that humans have never known before. We're in an emotional and psychological state of displacement. It's an alternate reality that I found interesting to explore.

In *The Global Soul*, I write a lot about traveling, but I've also been working on another book which is about spending time in a monastery, something I've done quite a lot of in the last ten years. It's a kind of a companion piece to *The Global Soul* about sinking roots, just being surrounded by silence and ocean and sky, and traveling without leaving a room.

In Japan, I live in a little neighborhood in the middle of nowhere. I don't have a bicycle or a car or anything, so my only movement is within the boundaries of my feet. I feel there's a need for that kind of conscientious objection to the momentum of the world.

Dave: The parallels and allusions to *Walden* and Thoreau are interesting for me, especially toward the end when you talk about rooting yourself in an environment that presents very little that's familiar to you. You almost achieve the Walden-like state Thoreau wrote about, that degree of simplicity, but you've clearly made a conscious effort not to assimilate yourself more thoroughly into Japanese culture.

Iyer: It's a way of filtering. Because I speak only rudimentary Japanese, I can't watch t.v., I can't read the newspaper, I can't engage in chit chat. Cut away all those externals and distractions.

In the past, most of the books I've written have been broadly categorized as travel books because they're about the adventure and excitement of seeking out foreign places. This book is about travel not as a quest or a pilgrimage, but as a way of life among people who have to do it. Merchants, for example, who have always moved from door to door the way traveling salesmen do, but now have to wake up in summer and fly across the world and sleep that same night in winter. The global economy is making them global beings.

"Globalization" has become the great tag phrase, but when we talk about it, it's nearly always in terms of the global marketplace or communications technology, either data or goods that are whizzing around. We forget that people are whizzing around more and more. On them, it takes a toll.

The life of Thoreau has always exerted a great attraction to many people in many different societies. It seems there are more and more people, even while they're conducting regular lives, who are deciding that they have to clear out more space for themselves.

Thoreau is at the secret heart of this. When you're lost in one of those secret passageways in Hong Kong, it's easy to forget that's what underneath.

Dave: An essay of yours, "Why We Travel," was included in *The Best Spiritual Writing 1999*. You write:

> Travel is the best way we have of rescuing the humanity of
> places and saving them from abstraction and ideology.

That idea seems elemental to your ideal of what a multicultural city like Toronto can strive to be.

Iyer: It's the case in Portland, but certainly in San Francisco, Los Angeles, Seattle, or New York, that even someone who has never left the city is surrounded by many languages she can't read and customs she can't follow. All the remotest parts of the world are suddenly at her front door. People are traveling even if they've never left their home town. All of us, whether we move or not, are having to deal with this crossing of cultures.

In America, where the economy is prospering, there's a sense that the doors being opened by technology are very exciting. It gets easier and easier to forget that ninety-seven percent of the people who are about to enter the world are dirt poor and they need just the most fundamental things: food, shelter, and safety.

Sometimes we get so excited by the possibilities of the Net, for example—which does help bring health and educational support to people—but in our relatively privileged places we forget that in Cambodia, for example, where I was last year, what they most need is a mosquito net. I was told that if you spend five dollars, you can save three lives in Cambodia. Technology is a wonderful thing, but in most places I visit the needs are much more urgent and age-old.

One of the strange things that seems to be happening as we get more wired is not that the world is getting smaller, but that in some ways I feel the distances are expanding. We're only caught up in the illusion of smallness. A tiny part of the world is becoming very rich and mobile while the rest is more deeply entrenched in its problems than ever.

Dave: You use Hong Kong as an example of a place where you can be a plane-hopping, mobile person, traveling all the time, and still never see anything. 6.2 million people live in Hong Kong, you write, and of them, six million are Chinese. But your friend, who lives in what's basically a complete city unto itself with living quarters, shopping, food, entertainment, and a connection to the airport—a place you call "a kind of floating International Settlement"—never sees any of those Chinese.

Iyer: Yes, a traveler can screen out more and more of the world unless he takes particular pains to go to those kinds of places. But we can get these lessons in our own cities, of course—if you just take the wrong subway train in New York, you're certainly reminded of what's happening outside privileged Manhattan. Or if you walk around the Capitol late at night in D.C.

At some level, people are more exposed to other cultures and know more about them than ever before. Here in Portland, people can eat Thai food, they know about Tibetan Buddhism, they may have met an Ethiopian, all kinds of things that were inconceivable only twenty years ago. At the surface level, we're all much more cosmopolitan, but at the level of conscience, I'm not so sure—just as in the example of the Hong Kong expatriate.

Dave: You do like Toronto a lot, though. It's not perfect, but Toronto seems to represent the hope you have for how cities might develop.

Iyer: Yes, partly because the government is very self-consciously and earnestly trying to draft what is essentially a multicultural bill of rights. Canada, in general, and Toronto, in particular, is small enough and malleable enough to be shaped into a workable international community.

The other reason why I was drawn to Toronto initially was that every few months I'd get a book through the mail, and it would be the most exciting and unprecedented book I'd run into. When I looked at the back, it seemed the author was always from Toronto.

Michael Ondaatje is the obvious example. But Anne Michaels and so many others who are making this new Canadian literature—and Canadian literature is as resurgent as any, though it's being made largely by people from Tanzania and India, Sri Lanka, The West Indies, and other places—many of these authors are imaginatively trying to construct new notions of a community beyond nations, as in *The English Patient*, where just at a time when nationalism is most intense, during World War II, and people are being killed because of nationalities, these four individuals exist, as it were, in a desert where all distinctions are dissolved.

Toronto seems, in certain small, practical ways, to be trying to fashion a new sense of order, how to make a peace between cultures, and its writers seem to sense that they're living in the midst of something very exciting. Also, of course, Toronto is the birthplace of the Global Village—that's where McLuhan wrote about it.

It should also be said that whenever I pose this theory to Torontonians they're pretty surprised. They're much more skeptical about the city than I am. But statistically, it's the most multicultural city in the world. According to the UN, it's the safest city in North America, and it's generally regarded as one of the cities in North America that works best. It's also the most mongrel. When you put those things together, it offers a very hopeful prospect of how the city of the future will come into being.

Toronto provides a counterpoint, in my prejudiced opinion, to Los Angeles, for example, or Atlanta.

Dave: Ha Jin visited recently. We talked a bit about Atlanta. I think he'd agree with much of what you write about it in *Global Soul.*

Iyer: Did you enjoy *Waiting* [Jin's prize-winning novel]?

Dave: I did. More than anything else, I guess, it was just so different from anything else I normally read.

Iyer: And so different from our experience, too. It's incomprehensible, those lives. But I was a little surprised that it did as well as it did.

Dave: It was surprising, but he tells a great story, and I think the style was just so fresh and shocking. It was so devoid of the clutter that ends up in most novels now.

Iyer: In that sense, very Chinese, reflective. The minimalist background.

What's interesting to me about Atlanta is that, on paper, it's one of the forces that makes the global economy go round. It's the home of CNN, Coca-Cola, Delta, Holiday Inn, and UPS, and yet in reality it seems utterly locked in those old black and white divisions, in every sense.

You're standing outside Martin Luther King's birthplace on Auburn Avenue and the whole neighborhood around it is completely derelict and disenfranchised, then a ten-minute walk from there you run into all the gleaming towers and convention centers and seventy-story hotels. It's poignant. But a lot of the world is beginning to look like that: a few futuristic towers linked into the global economy and, around them, wasteland.

Dave: The chapter in *The Global Soul* about the Olympics was one of my favorites. I read passages to my roommate, who used to live in Atlanta and just moved here from Salt Lake, two cities made-over for the Games. I loved the story about those archers from Bhutan who arrive in Barcelona and are absolutely blown away by how different things are from their homeland, the only place they'd ever known.

The new allegiances are corporate, though, not national. Michael Jordan threatened not to stand in front of the flag if he couldn't wear his Nikes and it's not uncommon for an athlete to compete on behalf of a country that's thousands of miles from his or her actual home.

Iyer: The Olympics is really stranded on that shift. It's based on national divisions which, to some extent, have ceased to exist. Kenyans turn into Danes so as to enhance their chances of winning a medal.

Dave: Torontonians may not agree with your idealistic view of their city, but you also mention Haruki Murakami and his novel, *The Wind-up Bird Chronicle*. Murakami, who's Japanese, doesn't agree with your idealistic view of Japan at all. The point being that any native tends to be more cynical about his own culture.

Iyer: I think I say in the book that a foreigner tends to see paradise where a native sees purgatory, insofar as a foreigner is in a privileged position and has more appreciative eyes, undimmed by familiarity.

It's the case for me, too: I was born in England, and England is the one country in the world that will never have any glamour for me.

Dave: I was entertained by the various literary references in the book. It seems like you spend an awful lot of your time reading.

Iyer: I do have the advantage of living in the middle of nowhere. In Japan, I know my girlfriend, but otherwise I have very little contact. It's a good place for reading and writing, for being calm, and following those pursuits. I do review books, as well. And I read for pleasure, but principally, I'm drawn to books that are likely to speak to me.

One of the exciting things now is that more and more of the prominent books around us are written by mongrels about the interaction between multicultured beings and multicultured cities. Whether it's Kazuo Ishiguro, Ondaatje, Salman Rushdie, or Derek Walcott, so many of the figures who are dominant in the world of the novel or poetry are wrestling with these issues because they've been uprooted, themselves.

For example, I think a lot of the great writers on globalism, imaginative writers, are from India. That's partly because people who grow up in India tend to be multiculturalists, already—they have three or four cultures, already. Whether you're talking about Rushdie, Bharati Mukherjee, Anita Desai, or Amitav Ghosh, all the famous Indian writers literally have feet in four or five different cultures and so have a sense of how this new internationalism is forming that those more rooted in traditional cultures don't. That, to me, reflects the new inner globalism that is a theme of this book.

And they're bringing a freshness. These writers from four corners of the universe who are working within English literature are flooding it with alien smells and curious words, different customs, and utterly

unprecedented rhythms. It's as if the stuffy old house of English literature has suddenly been given bright, tropical colors. Novels in our own
language now are as exciting as those of Garcia Marquez or those from
Africa. And that's all happened in the last twenty years or so.

Dave: You use The Booker Prize as an example of these trends. Most
of the recent winners have been writers like Ondaatje who fall under
the umbrella of the Commonwealth, but they're writing from a true
multiculturalist's perspective.

   You also talk about publicists measuring a book's success not by the
number of copies in print but by the number of languages it's
reached—the inevitable consequence of which is that those writers end
up spending more time in foreign places and therefore will write, in the
future, more about being in airports and hotels.

Iyer: Ishiguro says he's so conscious of an international audience that he
deliberately fashions his novels in a way that's easy to translate, and
without topical references, because he knows his readers are going to
meet him as much in Norwegian or Cantonese or Arabic as in English.

   From the minute he begins to conceive his novels, he's thinking of
the global audience, and in his case, hitting a universal chord, very
consciously aiming for that.

Dave: If an author writes with the understanding that two-thirds of
his audience will read his work in translation, there'd seem to be a risk
that he'd spend less time worrying about elements such as sentence
construction and voice. Do plot and theme threaten to take over?

Iyer: It depends what kind of writer you are. The two great writers of exile,
the two great paradigms, are Joyce and Beckett. Joyce lived in Dublin all his
life, imaginatively, and essentially suffuses the page with the most untrans-
latable stuff—every word is a pun spinning in many directions, rooted in

the texture of Dublin—whereas Beckett's work is very easy to translate, and I think he pretty much wrote it in two languages at once. He goes instantly to some human core that's apprehensible anywhere. I think Ishiguro is trying to do that, and it makes sense for his kind of writing. But it would be dangerous for a writer instantly to think of a global audience because he may be robbing himself of his own voice.

It's a very special writer who can write in a universal tongue. Ishiguro has the peculiar blessing of having grown up neither Japanese nor English. The English he writes is both more formal than a typical English person's and also a little strange. It has a curious flavor. At the same time, by his own admission, he can't even write Japanese. In some ways, inadvertently, he's reflecting that mongrel background, and that can't be forced.

Dave: What are you thinking about these days? You mentioned you're working on the complement or companion piece to *Global Soul*.

Iyer: Yes. I've been spending a lot of time at a Benedictine hermitage in California. I'm not Benedictine, but the brothers there are kind enough to open their doors to anyone who wants stillness.

Also, I'm writing a novel. One advantage of turning myself into a novelist is that I don't have to travel so much. I can sit at my desk in Japan and travel inwardly. It's set in California but stitched around Sufism, of all things, a sort of Persian mystery.

In *The Global Soul*, I'm writing about globalism because it's my inheritance, and the inheritance of so many people around the world. Globalism is the landscape of the new century, the world we're entering. Having done this book, now I want to go deeper into what people are going to be doing against that backdrop.

Dave: In the last chapter of this book, things do become much more quiet, more pensive and still.

Iyer: It's perhaps a pity that you have to wait until the last chapter to go there, but that chapter is a conscious attempt to make sense of everything that's gone before it, to give a counterpoint and a perspective.

The last chapter is rooted in one alien, but steadying, little community in the middle of Japan. I went all the way to Japan, and I found myself in this suburb which basically looks like the San Fernando Valley. There are none of the traditional props of Japan—no temples, no shrines, no narrow streets.

On the surface, it's another one of these rather soulless and impersonal places, and I deliberately write about it to emphasize the importance of not being distracted by the surface, keeping your eyes instead on what's essential, as Thoreau probably did better than anyone. Amidst alien surfaces you can certainly feel at home if you're surrounded by values or assumptions or priorities with which you're comfortable.

So the book begins with the burning house, with an account of my house in California literally burning to the ground, leaving me homeless. And it ends with me finding a home in this very alien place because I'm better appreciating that home has entirely to do with invisible, intangible qualities by which you guide your life. It has nothing to do with soil, really. As you said, there's a symmetry: the first chapter is called "The Burning House" and the last chapter is called "The Alien Home." It's a progression, from a house to a home.

The last chapter is the key. That's the chapter I like most, by far.

Pico Iyer visited Powell's City of Books on March 27, 2000. The Van Morrison CDs he can't seem to get out of his stereo lately are *Poetic Champions Compose; No Guru, No Method, No Teacher; Avalon Sunset*; and *The Philosopher's Stone*, disk one.

Joe Jackson Has Been Busy Making Other Plans

◆

A Cure for Gravity is Joe Jackson's love letter to music, the tell-all tale of an early infatuation which soon grew into a life-consuming obsession. With 1979's *Look Sharp!* and the succession of smart pop albums that followed, Jackson sold millions of records, but his book spends hardly ten pages on the lot of them. Now, twenty years after his debut album, he's just released his first symphony on the Sony Classical label—but he didn't write about that, either. Instead, *A Cure for Gravity* focuses on his early musical career, from childhood up to his twenty-fourth birthday.

Writing about his initial aspirations and the strange musical road that led a scrawny kid from "a gloomy place of soot-blackened brick and slag-heaps" to pop stardom, Jackson gives us an altogether different, humble rock story, one likely to please curious music audiences and emerging artists equally well. "A book about music thinly disguised as a memoir," as he calls it.

"Good critics are knowledgeable and passionate about their subjects, and motivated by a desire to help others enjoy them more," Jackson writes—about *music* critics. His first book about music more than meets that high standard.

Dave: Why write a book?

Joe Jackson: When I first started writing, it was therapy. I wanted to get some things out of my system, get some stories down on paper before I'd forgotten them all. In other words, I was just doing it for myself. By the time I got to the third draft, I was starting to think of it as being a book—but only at that point did I start thinking about a potential reader and a potential publisher. It went through six drafts.

There were actually many reasons. As I got further into it, I realized that I had a lot to say about music. This was giving me the opportunity to do it, as well as telling my own story because it's all so interrelated with music. After about thirty years as a musician, I felt that I'd earned the right to say a few things.

Dave: It doesn't pretend to be a biography.

Jackson: It's not.

Dave: It's more about one person's evolution as a musician than a typical rock biography.

Jackson: Right. It's not a rock biography at all. I tried very hard not to do that.

Dave: Reading it made me think a lot about the jobs I've had and the various forms of training I've had as a writer—the jobs any beginning artist takes to support his or her work, really. At one point, you took a job backing cabaret acts at The Playboy Club, for instance. It wasn't what you wanted to be doing, certainly, but it's impressive and fortifying to me how much you managed to glean about craft and showmanship from those shows.

Jackson: Definitely. John Lennon once said that life is what happens when you're busy making other plans, which is really true. Everything goes into the pot, it becomes part of you.

Dave: Do you see direct influences from those jobs in your later work?

Jackson: I don't know how direct, but everything's an influence, really. When people ask what are my influences, it strikes me as a very difficult question. I'm influenced by everything, including things I hate. I might hear a piece of music I can't stand, but there could be three notes in there that spark something in my mind. Then it'll be so disguised and mutated by the time it turns into something of mine that it's hard to tell where it came from.

Dave: What about as an author? Were there books you used as guides or some style you had in mind?

Jackson: Not when I started. The third draft was the most difficult part of this—about halfway through the writing—because I realized that I didn't have a voice, which is this really cliché thing, right? Every writer's trying to find a voice. But it struck me that I was trying to be too clever, and I needed to simplify it.

One of the things, though, that really did help me was reading a book of interviews with Graham Greene. He was always one of my favorite writers, and I think I've probably read most of his books. He said that when he was writing he would always, at regular intervals, read out loud from what he had written. I started doing that and it was incredibly helpful. It helped me find a conversational tone. Greene's idea was that if there was a false note in the writing, it would be really obvious when you read it out loud.

It's true. I started thinking of it as if I weren't writing a book at all; I was just talking to a bloke in a pub. That was very helpful.

Dave: The book recounts the quest to find your *musical* voice. What it really brings out is how one person reaches that point of understanding. Because you certainly didn't get there directly. Maybe no one does.

Jackson: No, I had to swim through many rivers of shit, but the great thing is that now I can be very smug and say, "Oh, I paid my dues." So it works out!

I wanted to write an accessible and entertaining book with some serious things to say, as well, but not beating anyone over the head with it. It's amazingly easy to come across as being pompous or didactic. I had people reading my earlier drafts telling me that I was coming across that way, and I was horrified. But it doesn't take much to get those accusations flowing.

Dave: Your fans might be interested to hear your personal story, but there's a lot more to the book than that. The story speaks to anyone interested in what it takes or what it's like to earn a living from a career in art.

Jackson: I wanted it to be accessible to non-musicians without being boring to musicians. But I think fans would enjoy it.

Dave: You don't talk about *Look Sharp!* until the next-to-last chapter. But throughout *Cure for Gravity*, you open many of the chapters in the present, in the mid-nineties, which constantly grounds the reader in that retrospective position. Because of that, even though you've skipped the intervening years, it's easy for a reader to make the leap and understand how you've gotten to where you are now. It worked for me. Was that a structural device you had in mind from early on?

Jackson: It was another thing that evolved. I used the structure of a memoir as a framework on which to hang ideas about music and, in a way, a manifesto. In other words, saying, "This is what I'm all about."

Talking about the first twenty-four years of my life turned out to be a good way to do that, as opposed to talking about what came after that, which I think is quite boring, actually. It's the same old story: touring and recording, touring and recording, having parties, taking drugs…

Dave: Toward the end, you talk about letting "Joe Jackson, the Pop Star" die. Did that take a long time?

Jackson: It was a struggle, yeah.

Dave: Because you've taken a step that many musicians don't or can't make. You're still a musician, a recording artist.

Jackson: I'm still writing stuff that has a lot of pop elements, too. It's not inaccessible to people who like pop music. All I did was make a conscious decision to step away from the rules and regulations of the pop world. I stopped thinking in terms of singles and airplay and radio formats and charts and all the rest. Now, I'm having a really good time. It's actually fresh and exciting again.

Dave: Is it money? Is it ego? To walk away from that position and say that's not important anymore, to say you don't need to be on MTV every third hour, and do what you want to do?

Jackson: I don't really not *need* to be on MTV; I don't *want* to be on MTV anymore. I think it's not so much about money—although some people have one hit and get themselves ridiculously into debt; I never did that—but I'm not sure it's really about money for many people. I think, as you say, it's more about ego. Needing to fill some kind of emptiness in your life with success and adulation. It's unfortunate because even when it happens, it rarely lasts very long, no matter who you are or what you do. In a way, success makes things even worse when it's gone.

I think it's very important for every artist to have your own definition of what success is, to be very clear about it, because, otherwise, you're in trouble. The pop world defines success in very big terms. Because there are a few people who sell ten million albums, record companies feel like everyone should. If you sell one or two hundred thousand, they can make you feel like a failure. And that's not bad, to sell a hundred thousand albums! It's not bad to sell ten thousand, or ten, for that matter. And that's one of the reasons I wanted to get out of pop.

The last album I made for Virgin sold about a hundred fifty or two hundred thousand copies, which, considering the kind of record it was and the fact that it wasn't promoted very well, is actually pretty good, I thought. But as far as they were concerned, it was a failure because Janet Jackson was about to come out and she was going to sell five million.

I had to get away from that. I don't want to walk around feeling like I'm a failure for making a record that I'm proud of and selling a couple hundred thousand copies of it. That's just crazy.

Dave: *Symphony No. 1* is on the Sony Classical label. How is that different for you?

Jackson: It's my second record with them. We have an interesting and, in some ways, experimental partnership. Their agenda is to broaden what a classical label can do. Peter Gelb, the head of Sony Classical, whom I greatly admire, is smart enough to know they've sold about as many copies of Beethoven's *Fifth* as they ever will. What are they going to do now? His idea is that a label like Sony Classical can reach out and embrace music which is eclectic or doesn't really fit, music that is a crossover in some way or another. Music that isn't pop.

They were excited about working with me, and when it comes down to it, I want to work with someone who wants to work with me. It's an interesting set-up because they're not coming from a pop mentality. To them, I'm helping them reach out to a broader audience.

It's a funny twist. To them, I'm a populist.

Dave: You made a conscious effort to be a populist when you were younger. You chose popular music over classical, which was really your first love.

Jackson: At one point, I did—when I was younger and more arrogant.

But I think it's okay for an artist to have some diversity, and that's a hard sell these days. If something's harder to market, you'll just hear, "Oh, there's no audience for it." Of course, there is. I don't see any reason why a composer can't write songs in a more or less popular idiom and also write a symphony. Plenty of people have done exactly that. If it's a hard sell, tough shit.

Dave: It's the exact same situation in the book industry, of course. If a book isn't easily marketable and the big chains can't sell a gluttonous number of copies, it's highly unlikely that it will even get published. It's just the same.

Jackson: Exactly. I had a terrible time getting this published in the States. In the UK, I got a really good publisher almost immediately, but in the States I had a lot of trouble for exactly that reason. I got a pile of letters from editors, every one of which says that they love the book, but none of them would commit to publishing it. Because it doesn't quite fit one category or the other. And the thing is, if it had been a really trashy pop star biography and I had a big hit record at the time, they'd snatch it right up. That's a fact. It's depressing, but I try not to take it personally.

Dave: When you play live now, what kind of stuff do you play? I saw on your web site that you'd recorded some very small shows in New York.

Jackson: There's a live album coming out in February, hopefully. We just finished mixing it. It has some new versions of old songs and some cover versions, as well, which might surprise some people.

Dave: Care to give some examples?

Jackson: Then they wouldn't be surprises, now, would they?

Dave: There's a great scene in your book when you talk about your first-ever lead vocal, singing "When I'm Sixty-Four." Just the image of it…

Jackson:…with the microphone taped onto a folding music stand, falling over.

Dave: The band didn't let you do the lead vocals again after that.

Jackson: No, it was bad.

Dave: You're still playing with a lot of the same people who were in bands with you in your teens and early twenties.

Jackson: Well, "still playing" implies that there's some kind of ongoing thing, which there isn't—everything is on a project-by-project basis—but the same names do crop up over and over again. Certain people, they're very good, and they're versatile enough to deal with the various things I do. And they're friends, as well.

Dave: Do you have any ideas about what direction your career might take in the future?

Jackson: No, I don't have an agenda or a plan that's more than a year ahead. The next album I'm doing is more of a song-oriented one. Really, I'll just continue building this body of work, or whatever you want to call it. I'll definitely write another symphony. But it's not like I have a checklist of Things I Want to Do.

Dave: Do you want to write more?

Jackson: Yeah, I don't know what it will be, though. But I want to do more just because I enjoy it so much. Now, people are telling me that I write well. Who knew? But I think I did a decent job. My publisher in England says I should write a novel, but I don't know. There are only so many things you can do without falling on your ass.

I met with Joe Jackson above the Annex prior to his appearance at the City of Books on December 1, 1999. It's safe to say he signed more album covers (not CDs, mind you, but records) for Powell's employees than any other recent visiting author. What's more, Joe proved to be as tall as my friend (and coworker) Darin had led me to believe.

"Joe Jackson?" Darin had asked, eavesdropping on my phone call. "The musician?"

"That was his publicist," I told him. "He's coming to Powell's, apparently. He's written a book."

"One of the tallest stars in rock and roll history," Darin said.

"Tall and sharp," I reminded him. "Tall and *sharp*."

We crack ourselves up here, we really do.

Gish Jen Passes Muster—Again

◆

William Faulkner, Ernest Hemingway, Flannery O'Connor, Willa Cather…forty-one of the fifty-five authors represented in *Best American Short Stories of the Century* wrote their award-winning piece before 1980. A grade school in my home town was named after Hemingway. As far as I know, there is no such thing as Gish Jen Elementary School, anywhere, yet here she is alongside Papa in the century-ending collection. Her story, "Birthmates," originally published by *Ploughshares* in 1995, was deemed worthy by editors John Updike and Katrina Kenison.

Having published two novels, *Typical American* and *Mona in the Promised Land*, Jen came to Powell's to introduce her first collection of shorter, award-winning pieces. It was refreshing to talk about short stories for a change. Any time you have the chance to read an author's work four or five times before meeting her, you can't help but feel better prepared.

"Updike once wrote a review of a Philip Roth novel in which he said that the novel had been 'a little too long in the writing' and that, as a result, all these offshoots had sprung up. I think that's true: if it takes too long, your interest begins to wander," Jen admitted. "What I do with those side interests is I channel them into stories."

Dave: When did you find out that "Birthmates" had been chosen for *Best American Short Stories of the Century*?

Gish Jen: It's over a year ago now, but I was completely shocked. Updike is the kind of writer that I would want to be respected by, but I don't think he's the type I write for. This is a terrible thing to say, but I wouldn't have thought that my world and my concerns would resonate with him. I was just completely shocked and thrilled to find out I was entirely wrong.

Dave: This is your first collection of stories, but you've been writing and publishing them for a while. Another story in *Who's Irish?*, "The Water-Faucet Vision," was selected by Mark Helprin for *Best American Short Stories 1988*. And another, "In the American Society," is already anthologized in college textbooks.

Jen: I'd been thinking for some time of doing a collection, and when I got pregnant with my new child, I knew it wasn't time to start another novel. Also, I had a number of stories that had been hanging around for a while. But there was something about that second trimester of pregnancy—I don't know, my estrogen levels were really high—but for one reason or another I started writing stories.

Three of these pieces came quite quickly. I finished "House House Home," I wrote "Duncan in China," and I wrote "Who's Irish?" all within a month and a half, which for me is very, very fast.

By the time I had those pieces, I knew I had a collection. I was still hoping to make an aesthetic whole. You want to have the collection cohere. I wasn't sure I had that before.

Dave: The stories feel like the work of one author, certainly, but at the same time, there are a lot of different points of view, different structures. No two of the stories feel the same, which is rare for a collection.

Jen: I wrote almost all these stories while I was supposed to be doing something else, so they're all off the beaten track for me. I don't know if that accounts for the variety or not.

Updike once wrote a review of a Philip Roth novel in which he said that the novel had been "a little too long in the writing" and that, as a result, all these offshoots had sprung up. I think that's true: if it takes too long, your interest begins to wander.

What I do with those side interests is I channel them into stories. That's good because it enables me to go back to my novel and not be distracted. But also, by their nature, they compel you to write them— without realizing it, you are. So maybe more than a novel could be, they're products of your unconscious. There's a kind of waywardness to them; maybe it's not surprising that they would be extremely various.

Dave: Because you didn't sit down to write a bunch of stories.

Jen: Yes, they're all things that came unprompted.

Dave: In the notes to *Best American 1995*, you say you wrote "Birthmates" while you were writing *Mona in the Promised Land*.

Jen: One thing I've noticed is that if I'm writing something very funny, it tends to engender something which is serious. I think every writer struggles to keep that opposite tendency in check so the novel doesn't take a big right turn and become something else. But with "Birthmates" I got it out of my system; I wrote the story and went back to work on *Mona*.

Dave: "Birthmates" has a completely different tone than *Mona*, but it's pretty funny. It's safe to say that to be considered for *Best American of the Century*, a story has to be complex enough that you can read it a few times and still be getting more out of it. For me, in the case of "Birthmates," it's two things: point of view and the balance between the serious context and the really funny passages in the middle of it all.

A bunch of the lines stand out: "The tie pin was smiling. The man was not." The sign behind the hotel registration desk that reads, "FEWEST

CUSTOMER INJURIES, 1972-73." And just the whole idea of a man walking around all day carrying a phone as an instrument of self-defense.

Jen: Yeah, he's walking around his hotel with his phone. He's armed with a telephone handset. It's funny. But it's a different kind of humor than *Mona*. There's not as much vocal humor in the story as there is in *Mona*, but there's a lot of situational humor.

Early on in my career people would say, "Is this supposed to be funny or it supposed to be sad?" And I would hear voices like that and think that somehow I was supposed to resolve my work, be either funny or sad. Then at a certain point I finally decided, for better or worse, I was somebody who simultaneously sees things as happy *and* sad. I am the kind of person who would make a joke on someone's deathbed, tacky as it may seem.

It could be seen as an Asian part of my sensibility, in the sense that it's a very Asian thing to imagine that opposites go together. Ying-yang, sweet and sour. There isn't the sense that something should be sweet *or* sour, one or the other. I don't know if that's completely true, but in any case that ying-yang quality certainly embodies a lot of these stories.

Dave: You mention in the notes also that a lot of the emotion came from a terminated pregnancy of your own—and the whole idea of being able to laugh or creating an environment where you could laugh.

Jen: It took me years. The pregnancy that I lost came while I was writing *Typical American*, and in some ways I think it accounts for why the ending of that book is so sad. I lost the pregnancy between the fourth and fifth sections. People will analyze and analyze, but the experience changed me. I was very worried I wouldn't finish that book because I was a different person. It was my first pregnancy, conceived after a long period of infertility.

But I did finish *Typical American*, and that experience kind of sat there with me all through *Mona*. Then all of a sudden, almost at the end of *Mona*...obviously, their marriage was not my marriage and those facts are not my facts (the way they lose their child is actually not the way I lost my child), but the fact was that I knew what it was to lose a pregnancy. And the fact that I could write about it with anything like levity represented a kind of maturing that had taken me, what, six years to achieve?

Dave: And yet essentially you present it from his point of view, the husband's. It's third-person, but it's sitting with him.

Jen: It's sitting with him. The story in many ways is about his distance from it and his inability to close that distance.

In some ways, too, it's about a subtle fallout from racism. I realize that I was suggesting that Art Woo, in order to deal with his work environment, has had to deaden himself in certain ways. And the ways in which he's deadened himself have cost him his marriage.

Dave: I found it interesting. One the one hand, I'm reading and I sympathize with Art because he's not in a good situation; he's not in a comfortable environment. Yet at the same time when I look carefully, I see past his point of view to Lisa, who sees things completely differently. You show the reader her perspective by Art's trying to reconstruct it— what Lisa must have been thinking. Obviously he's failing to understand certain things; we see through his thoughts to something closer to the truth. But it's written in very casually. That's an interesting, effective, and very subtle way to build numerous viewpoints.

Jen: Well, thank you. She is kind of stitched in there lightly, kind of the way the daughter in "Who's Irish?" is stitched in, with just a couple of lines.

In my mind, I'm not on the side of either one of these characters. I think that she has a viewpoint and he has a viewpoint. She hasn't had to grapple with some of the hard realities he's had to deal with. It's not as though I see her as right. I see her as having learned to retain some of the humanity, but also as naive in some ways.

Dave: When he gets hit by the phone and collapses…that scene is building, though we don't know toward exactly what, then—*bam!*—all of a sudden he's down on the floor. I think it takes two lines. The whole scene, if you compare, mimics Lisa's recollection of the lightning. The first time I read the story, I didn't really notice. It's not heavy-handed.

Jen: I do hope there will be layers and layers of things for people to find. There are references and jokes along the way. Did you get the Oscar Wilde reference?

Dave: No.

Jen: Maybe next time.

Dave: For some reason, at odd moments throughout the day, I've found myself thinking of the passage about croissants. I can almost imagine Updike writing it—though I don't know if the comparison would have occurred to me if he hadn't been the one to choose the story for *Best of*.

> In truth, he had always considered the sight of men eating croissants slightly ridiculous, especially at the beginning, when for the first bite they had to maneuver the point of the crescent into their mouths. No matter what a person did, he ended up with an asymmetrical mouthful of pastry, which he then had to relocate with his tongue to a more central location. This made him look less purposive than he might. Also, croissants were more apt than other breakfast

foods to spray little flakes all over one's clean dark suit. Art himself had accordingly never ordered a croissant in any working situation, and he believed that attention to this sort of detail was how it was that he had not lost his job like many of his colleagues.

It might just be the word *purposive* that makes me think of Updike, I don't know why.

Jen: That's very flattering to me. I do pay close attention to the texture of life, which I suppose is Updike-like. But Updike is sort of a preternatural...

Dave: What do you read?

Jen: I just finished a wonderful book called *Return of the Soldier* by Rebecca West. I loved it. And I've been reading *Preston Falls* and liking it a lot.

Dave: I haven't read that yet, but I keep hearing about it lately. Our graphics guy told me that it was written by the former lead singer of Bread.

Jen: What?

Dave: They have the same name, the guy who wrote that book and the singer/songwriter in Bread: David Gates.

Jen: The author isn't the singer, though, right?

Dave: No. It's just another rumor, like Mikey died from Pop Rocks. Clyde was just screwing with me, and I fell for it.

Jen: Oh. Because I hadn't heard that.

Dave: We must be hanging out on different playgrounds.

Anyway, more than once you've written about Asian children adopting the religion of their American friends. In "The Water-Faucet Vision," it's Catholicism, and it's Judaism in *Mona*.

Jen: It's funny because everybody thinks of me as Jewish now. But, yes, I've also written about turning Catholic.

Dave: You've covered a lot of holy ground.

Jen: After *Mona* came out, so many people would come up to me and say, "What are you doing for the High Holidays?" And I'd say, "Um, I'm not Jewish." And I'd feel guilty. I'd feel like a lapsed Jew.

But "The Water-Faucet Vision" is about turning Catholic. It's also about superstition, that story. Religion is one more way the girls can define themselves.

Of course I'm interested in the Asian-American experience. But I'm also interested in architecture; I'm interested in religion. I'm very interested in the different realities, not just my own ethnic group. In *Mona*, I wrote extensively about what it means to be Jewish. And I was happy about that. That's one of the greatest challenges as a writer that I set for myself, to see that through effort and imagination you can penetrate another people's experience.

The bar is higher now than it used to be, which I think is a good thing; you can't get away with a so-so job when you're writing about an ethnic group other than your own. And I was very happy when Cynthia Ozick reviewed it and presented, really, a banner take. I was thrilled just to have attracted the notice of a writer whom I admire as much as I admire Cynthia Ozick. But in addition I was thrilled to have passed muster with her. I felt as if I had contributed in a tiny way to peace and understanding. And if I could do that, surely other people could imagine the Asian-American experience.

Gish Jen swung through town with her family on June 17, 1999. After her appearance in the City of Books, we browsed the Pacific Northwest section for a guide to Mount Saint Helens, where she'd be heading in the morning with her kin.

Ha Jin Lets It Go

♦

Xuefei Jin, known to readers as Ha Jin, began writing in English barely twelve years ago.

If he'd gone back to China, he says, he wouldn't be writing fiction or poetry—and he had every intention of returning to his native country as he prepared his dissertation at Brandeis University. After watching televised coverage of the Tiananmen Square massacre, however, Jin and his wife decided to make a life with their son here in the United States, and when Jin couldn't find teaching work, he turned to writing, instead.

Taking odd jobs (a night watchman, a busboy) until eventually his publishing success convinced Emory University to hire him to teach and write, Jin was arguably one of the most prolific literary writers of the nineties, producing two books of poetry ("This is a profound book, an event," Frank Bidart said of Jin's 1990 volume, *Between Silences*, his debut), two collections of short stories, and two novels. In the process, he earned a PEN/Hemingway prize (1996, for *Oceans of Words*, his first story collection) and The Flannery O'Connor Award for Fiction (1997, for *Under the Red Flag*, his second). Most recently, *Waiting* won both the 1999 National Book Award and the 2000 PEN/Faulkner Award for Fiction.

"I think the ultimate goal for a piece of literature is to transcend time to some degree, not to vacate it but to go through it," Jin explained. "To see past it to what is essential to the characters." His latest novel, like the rest of his incredible body of work, does just that.

Year after year, Lin Kong returns to his village to divorce his wife, and every year, without the divorce, he returns to the city and his lover, a nurse at the hospital where he has worked all his adult life. The government will not grant him a divorce without his wife's consent until they have been separated for at least eighteen years.

Waiting is a perfect antidote to our frantic, gotta-get-it-done-yesterday lives.

Dave: I was wondering where the idea for *Waiting* came from, where that story was born.

Ha Jin: The book is based upon a true story. Not exactly the same, but similar. My wife knew the doctor and the nurse. They both served in the hospital where my parents were army doctors. It was during a visit to my parents-in-laws, my first visit, that I heard this story.

Dave: *Waiting* is very different from most of what I read—and, to a certain extent, from most of what gets published and read today in the United States. You truly enter that Chinese world right from the start; it's unimpeachable, vividly alive.

Jin: The narrator is very close to things and events. Good writers should observe and tell the story, try to reveal the complexities, the subtleties, to tell what's happening. The narrator shouldn't be intrusive. You have to respect the intelligence of the reader. The reader will always have their own interpretations.

For me, my job was just to tell the story. To fulfill the story. Yes, in a way, there are a lot of irrelevant details, culturally bound references, but if they're not essential to the story, I should let them go.

Dave: One critic talked about "the personal being political" in your novels. Fundamentally, though, *Waiting* isn't political. It's about people: Lin, Manna, and Shuyu.

Jin: No, politics is only a context. The focus is on the person, the inner life, the life of the soul and how that changes, how the emotional life is affected by time and also by environment.

Dave: A lot has been made of the fact that you didn't learn to write in English until eleven or twelve years ago, and yet you've been very productive: two novels, two books of stories, and two books of poems.

Jin: I've been lucky in that what I've written has not been wasted. Every book I've written has gone to print. And, you know, I was driven by a fear, an instinct of survival. I was hired as a teaching writer; I had to publish enough to keep my job.

Dave: How did you end up at Emory University?

Jin: No other places would hire me!

Dave: You're taking off from teaching right now, right?

Jin: Yes, on the Guggenheim Fellowship.

Dave: What are you teaching when you're there? Creative writing?

Jin: Most of the time, poetry writing, and occasionally fiction writing. Sometimes literature courses.

Dave: Are you still writing a lot of poetry, then?

Jin: Yes, I have a book coming out, in fact, this fall. It's called *Wreckage.*

Dave: How do you balance teaching with your own writing?

Jin: For me, teaching is a good way to make a living. Also, I think it gives me a kind of freedom that I might not have if I were a full-time writer. I'm willing to take risks. I'm less worried about how a book will sell. That helps. On the other hand, it's the same energy that I put into the students' work, into the preparation for the course. If you teach too much, you don't have the energy left, and energy is your main asset.

Dave: Do you work according to a set schedule? How much writing are you able to do?

Jin: When I teach a course I can't write as much as I'd like, but I try to write some every day. It doesn't have to be new—I edit, revise, just do something every day.

Dave: You studied Literature at Brandeis. Did you have a particular focus?

Jin: Poetry and poetics. I wrote my dissertation on modern poetry: Ezra Pound, T.S. Eliot, Auden, and Yeats. High modernists.

Dave: How did you come to focus on those particular poets?

Jin: Those four have poems which are related to Chinese texts and poems that reference the culture. My dissertation was aimed at a Chinese job market. I planned to return to China.

Dave: But after the Tiananmen Square massacre, you decided to stay here.

Jin: Yes, but it was too late to change my dissertation. I was completing it at the time.

Dave: If you'd gone back to China, if things had worked out differently, what do you think you'd be doing now?

Jin: Oh, I'd be a translator, I suppose. A critic.

Dave: Do you think you'd be writing novels?

Jin: No, I don't think so. Perhaps I might write one book or two, a memoir about my life, but not these kinds of books. There would be no pressure to write them.

Dave: So, in a way, the pressure is a good thing.

Jin: It's a mixed blessing. This is more meaningful for me. And it's something I can do.

Dave: Some people would say you do it well.

Jin: I don't know, but the page and the paper is something I can handle.

Dave: Is working in English becoming more natural for you?

Jin: I wouldn't say natural, but it's less difficult than in the beginning. Still now, stories take a long time to get finished, but the anxieties and uncertainties are slightly different than before.

Dave: The first story in *Under the Red Flag*, "In Broad Daylight," won the Pushcart Prize. It's a brutal story. *Waiting* is so much quieter.

Jin: It's very hard to keep that kind of intensity in a novel, if not impossible. You have to depend on the narrative voice, a different kind of rhythm.

Dave: And *Waiting* is very different even from *In the Pond* [Jin's previous novel, his first]. Did you want to try something different again or was it simply a case where the story demanded that you change the style?

Jin: It was just a different story. Tragic.

Dave: I really liked *In the Pond*. It's impressive that you pull off the humor across cultural boundaries. I don't know that I've read anything quite like it.

Jin: *In the Pond* is a comedy. A lot of people tell me it's their favorite. It's the kind of book you either hate it or you love it.

I had a really hard time selling it. Nobody would buy it. Comedy is a high order of art, very rare. Life is full of tragedies, but how can you write comedy without vulgarities? That's a huge handicap.

Dave: You entered the army at fourteen, right? Was that the standard age?

Jin: No. My father was an officer, so we had privileges. We could go into the army early. The standard age at the time, for our group, was sixteen. I lied. I told them I wasn't fourteen. I just wanted to leave home, to go away. There was nothing to do at home. Schools were closed.

Also, rumor had it that the Russians were going to attack, so I was scared. It was better to go to the army rather than stay at home waiting for an air raid.

Dave: How long were you in the army?

Jin: Five and a half years.

Dave: What did you imagine yourself doing? What did you see of your life then?

Jin: I saw very little. I wanted to read. In the beginning, I was basically illiterate. I couldn't read. Then in the second year the border calmed down. We knew there would be no war, we would live in peace, and I began to think of education. I wanted to go to college, to be a learned person, well-read.

Dave: Did that seem likely?

Jin: Yes. But my vision was very limited. Even the definition of *well-read* was different at the time. It was possible, as long as you worked hard. There were a lot of books. Bad books, but as long as you knew all of them, you were well-read!

Dave: Maybe my perspective is skewed, working on the Internet, but it's so hard now not to think globally. Every day, people in Prague and Auckland and hundreds of other cities in between are surfing our web site, whereas the outside world plays practically no role in *Waiting*. It's nonexistent to these people.

Jin: News is irrelevant to their life, that's true. That's how I perceived it. The book focuses on its framework and references to ground the story in a place and time, but other than that, I don't see the point in bringing up too many temporary references. I think the ultimate goal for a piece of literature is to transcend time to some degree, not to vacate it but to go through it. To see past it to what is essential to the characters.

Dave: In *Waiting*, a character quotes Beethoven: "Character is fate." That seems very appropriate to the novel.

Jin: Especially in the case of Lin Kong. Emotionally, he was crippled. He couldn't develop.

Dave: What starts the chain of events, to some degree, is the arranged marriage, but to a much greater degree it seems it's his whole life that's been arranged for him.

Jin: Yes, and he cooperated, unconsciously, with the arrangements. He internalized these laws into the fabric of his existence, so he's partially responsible as well.

Dave: You've mentioned elsewhere that you'll eventually write about the immigrant experience.

Jin: I haven't returned to China since I've been here. China is distant. I don't know what contemporary Chinese life is like now. I follow the news, but I don't have the mature sensation—I can't hear the noise, I can't smell the place. I'm not attached to it anymore. What's meaningful to me is the immigrant experience, the American life.

Dave: There's a long tradition of outstanding literature about the immigrant experience in America, of course. Are there any particular books or authors that stand out for you?

Jin: The best one, for me, is Nabokov's *Pnin*. I think that's the best. It deals with the question of language, and I think that's at the core of the immigrant experience: how to learn the language—or give up learning the language!—but without the absolute mastery of the language, which is impossible for an immigrant. Your life is always affected by the insufficiency.

Dave: A number of foreign books find their way into the hospital where Lin Kong and Manna Wu work. One of the characters in *Waiting* skips through the beginning of all the Russian novels because there's too much description. And you mention *Leaves of Grass* in here, too.

Jin: It's one of the great books, yes. Still, it's quite a well-respected, popular book among certain groups in China, even in the army. Officers did have access to it because Whitman was regarded as a proletarian poet.

Dave: Lin Kong has a personal library, and though he has to hide it, the books don't get taken away from him.

Jin: But he didn't use it. Gradually his life changed, and his library didn't function, especially after the marriage.

Dave: How common was it for people to have personal libraries stashed away?

Jin: Doctors in the army…there are all kinds of privileged people in the army. I saw highly literary officers reading Russian novels, the originals, hardcovers, filling bookcase after case. Many of the best writers in China now are from the army. It's not like here. There are a lot of privileges in army life if you can get into the right spot.

Dave: Have you taught about China or Chinese literature at all? Is that something you'd like to do?

Jin: For years, I looked for jobs related to Chinese literature or translation. But the applicants are very strong, all with degrees from American schools. A person like me, with no degree in Chinese, it's very hard for me to compete with them.

Dave: You're working on another novel now, right? What's that like?

Jin: Different, again. It's a first-person narrative. The language is slightly different, as well.

Dave: You plan to keep writing.

Jin: I think I've gone so far along this road that I can't just change. When I made the decision to write in English only, I was determined to travel all the way no matter how tough, how solitary it was. I have to go to the end, see what I can do.

Ha Jin visited Powell's City of Books on February 2, 2000 to read from *Waiting*. Before the appearance, before he browsed the shelves and before I took a picture of him in front of his books, he stopped by the Annex to talk.

Annie Leibovitz Puts Down Camera, Talks

◆

Name a few celebrities or artists. Annie Leibovitz has probably photographed them. Her brand new book presents one hundred seventy intimate portraits of women: teachers, soldiers, astronauts, miners, athletes, artists, executives, politicians, mothers, daughters—women. For the variety of lifestyles those pictures represent and the range of expression they capture, it likely will be remembered as the definitive photographic record of women at the turn of the century.

Before appearing at Powell's to meet her fans and sign copies of her new book, Annie talked about collaborating with Susan Sontag, who, in addition to contributing the essay which accompanies the pictures, first suggested the idea for *Women* and later helped choose its subjects. Annie described shoots on field trips across the country. She admitted her hesitancy to take on such a project and expressed the overwhelming gratification of seeing it through to completion.

She called herself "silly."

She also did a Eudora Welty impersonation that made that particular photograph completely come alive.

Dave: Some of the women in the new book are very well-known. Others aren't celebrities at all. How did you find the subjects?

Annie Leibovitz: There were a lot of lists made. Susan [Sontag] made a list. I made a list. I talked to John Rockwell at *The New York Times*. I talked to *Vogue* editors. Then there was this idea that there would be a set of field trips across the country.

I'd already shot the showgirls for *The New Yorker*, and I thought those made a really good set of pictures. I knew they would be good for the book. So I thought of a Muslim woman, a person who was the complete opposite of the showgirls, completely covering herself up. That was the start of the field trips. We went to a community outside of Detroit, a large Muslim community, and it was actually difficult getting women to sit, but one person agreed.

As the shoots continued over the last three years, especially toward the end when I didn't know if I was going to postpone the book, it was really a process of taking the pictures and putting them into a layout form, looking and seeing, How is this mix working? What am I missing? Toward the end, I thought I needed more women in manual labor. That's when I found the miners. I went out to California and shot the farmers. In local places, I found producers who might have ideas. And we'd look for events—if there was a tattoo convention or something.

We found subjects in every way you could possibly imagine. For example, I'd been trying for almost two years to get a shooting with Eudora Welty. Then I read the story in *The New York Times* about Osceola McCarty, the black washerwoman who gave all her money away—and she lives about a half hour away from Eudora.

Dave: It's funny that you mention those two women because they're actually two of my favorite pictures in the book. For me, the older women seem to resonate so much. Especially Eudora Welty. It's such a fantastic picture.

Leibovitz: It was so hard to get that shooting. When I finally got down to Mississippi, I was walking out the door to go meet her and I heard the phone ring. I didn't pick it up. She'd cancelled several times, and I was worried she'd be canceling again. They didn't know if she was well enough.

I was told she would come downstairs, sit in a blue chair, and I would have a few minutes. That was going to be it. But it was just getting to be spring, it was really beautiful outside, so I asked, "Would you like to go outside?"

Her helper looked at me with such a stern expression, smoke coming out of the ears, and Eudora said, "Yes! I would love to!" She put a coat on, went outside, and sat on her porch, which is where we shot it.

She was very, very Southern in her hospitality and politeness, saying, "I don't know why you want to take my picture!" There were so many good photographs from that shooting, it was hard to pick one.

Dave: There are a lot of very powerful women in the book who aren't necessarily celebrities.

Leibovitz: They're very well-known in their worlds. There are famous people in the book, but they became less important; the idea was to fold them in. Most are role models in some way.

Dave: You come from a background of journalism. It seems like that would be incredibly helpful on a project like this.

Leibovitz: The truth is, I thought I was doing journalism, but I really wasn't. At the San Francisco Art Institute, what I really studied was reportage, personalized reportage, *a la* Robert Frank and Cartier Bresson. I didn't know this, but it had a more personal slant. When I started working for *Rolling Stone*, I became very interested in journalism and thought maybe that's what I was doing, but it wasn't true. What became important was to have a point of view.

That's why I ended up using the title "Portrait Photographer." In a portrait, you have room to have a point of view and to be conceptual with a picture. The image may not be literally what's going on, but it's representative.

There was definitely an attempt in this book to be as straightforward as possible, but there are instances where to get the picture I want, I'm helping it.

For instance, Osceola: when I got there, she was sitting, waiting, all ready. And she was wearing her red suit and her wig, which she'd acquired since all of her notoriety. I walked around her house. It was very small. In her bedroom, her day dress was hanging on the back of a door.

I said, "Do you wear this?"

She said, "I wear it every day."

I asked, "Would you mind putting it back on?" Then I asked her if she would take the wig off. A true journalist doesn't have the right to ask that, but if you're illustrating, you can.

Dave: There are people in the book that you've photographed many times. Was the picture of Yoko Ono done specifically for this book?

Leibovitz: Yes, it was. I photographed her face many years ago, right after John died, within the year, I think. It was a very emotional, sad face. That photograph is in the 1983 book [*Photographs*]. I thought it would be interesting to revisit her and do her face, close up, one more time. She has a very strong Japanese face. I wanted to do an updated version.

About eighty percent was shot for the book.

Dave: It must have been hard taking these photographs knowing the context in which they'd be presented. It seems like a lot of responsibility.

Leibovitz: When I started, I was sincerely scared. The whole thing was very daunting. Where do you begin? How do you start? I was very scared of tackling this. It's such a big subject. I've said this before: I didn't want to let women down. But it became more about women's self-esteem. It really wasn't trying to be any kind of women's statement, but it became one on its own. Susan said this in her essay: some stereotypes are kept in place and some are broken.

You're very captivated by the older women. The more I look at the work, the more I realize that one of the stereotypes I see it breaking is the idea of aging and older women not being beautiful. It's not true.

But in terms of the responsibility, it's almost the reason I went ahead, why I didn't postpone the book. I was afraid I'd never finish it.

Dave: How involved was Susan Sontag in the process?

Leibovitz: It was her idea. I didn't jump right on the bandwagon. When I talked to my friends and other people I work with, they would get truly excited about it. I was glad they were excited and I thought it was interesting that they were excited, but no one really knew what the book was supposed to be. Who was supposed to be in it? Susan made one of the initial lists. I pulled it out recently, and I think we shot all fifteen of the women except one or two.

Even though she said she was going to write the essay, she didn't exactly a hundred percent agree until later. If she didn't like the book, I had a feeling I wasn't getting an essay. I kept thinking I'd wind up calling Joan Didion or something. *I wonder what Joyce Carol Oates is doing?* But it was important that she liked it, and she does have different tastes than I have.

When I first met her, she said, "You could be good," and I've always been trying to rise to that place.

Dave: When was that? When did you meet her?

Leibovitz: About eleven years ago. I met her to take her picture. She's been a great friend in my work, letting me be serious. I'd always felt like I had to be a little silly. Toward the end of this book, she told me, "You have to smarten this up a bit." She suggested Martha Nussbaum from the University of Chicago and Katha Pollitt from *The Nation*.

Dave: The first picture is of your mother. There's no picture of you.

Leibovitz: We ran out of time and space. We had more pictures than we could put in the book, and I was trying to hold the price down. It became the least important thing. There are people who really should be in this book and aren't. I thought about doing a self-portrait, but it didn't matter after a while because I couldn't run what I had.

Dave: Are there any pictures in the book that you're particularly proud of?

Leibovitz: I think the showgirls are really important. My favorite one is Susan McNamara, who looks almost like a librarian as herself. I hadn't planned to shoot them as themselves. I met them at Bally's and The Stardust after their shows, in their costumes. The idea was that they'd come to the studio and bring their costumes with them. When they showed up at the studio, I didn't recognize them. I thought it was incredible, the juxtaposition. I was very pleased with how it came out.

It's also an example of Susan Sontag's essay. She talks about how women, unlike men, dress up to be women. This is going beyond that in a way. In Susan McNamara's case, she's almost empowered by her costume, as if she's wearing armor.

Dave: They're powerful photographs, especially coming near the end of the book, all in a row.

Leibovitz: They're both intriguing—as the showgirls, I found them intriguing and beautiful, but then as themselves, that was also intriguing and beautiful to me.

Dave: How much time did you spend on these shoots? I'd imagine you spent a lot more time on the Natalie Portman shoot, for instance, than you might have on some of the others.

Leibovitz: Right. The Natalie Portman came out of a cover shoot, actually. For me, she filled the role of a young beauty, and I was trying to capture her place as a young girl becoming a woman. She's very young, but I almost thought, Oh, it's already too late to get the girl! She's already *Woman! Woman! Woman!* But I was trying to bring out the girl, too. She represented that to me more than an actress.

But, yes, that was done on a cover shoot for *Vanity Fair*, and it went on for a couple days down in Alabama. Interestingly enough, that's when I picked up the miners. We were going to Alabama and we just found that mine. It's a terrific story. We shot a half-mile down in the mining shaft. Those women are all married. The woman on the left hand side, Shirley, told me that she had worked twenty years in the mine because she'd put her four daughters through college. And we were all crying. It was those kinds of stories…

You were talking about the time we spent. These were done fast. They're not belabored, except when they're an assignment for a magazine. That's with the famous people. The unfamous, the unprofessional sitters, I've learned that it should be fast. It's either going to be good or it's not.

And of course what you're seeing in this book is the edit. Some of them didn't work. You can't make stuff work.

Dave: You've talked about one of the first big shoots you did, the one with John Lennon, how cooperative and straightforward he was and how much you appreciated that. You've become such a well-known figure since then. Is it any different for you now, being on the other end of it, especially when you're taking pictures of people who aren't quite as famous?

Leibovitz: I don't think most of them knew who I was, and it didn't really matter. I'd just ask if I could shoot them for my women's book. I think they were just excited to have their picture taken. But the truth is, most people, especially successful people, are hard working. They want to participate. They want to do things well.

What I learned from Lennon was something that did stay with me my whole career, which is to be very straightforward. I actually love talking about taking pictures, and I think that helps everyone. You're not there in the room talking to someone about something else while you're really trying to take their picture. You know, talking about the weather or the Knicks game because you're trying to pretend you're not really taking pictures. I always think that's funny. *We're not really taking pictures here! This will make you relax!* Lennon was very straightforward and helpful. What he taught me seems completely obvious: he expected people to treat each other well.

Dave: Do you have ideas about what you might do next?

Leibovitz: It's too soon for me to say what's the next idea, but I'm working on it. I'd like to do more books. This just wrapped, basically. There was a lot of work in printing it, and I've spent the last couple weeks talking about it. It's taken a lot of time. What's come out of all this is that I really like this book and this project. I didn't know when I did it how much I would like it. Now, one of the reasons I'm out talking about it is that I want to do more things like it.

Dave: We sent out a newsletter last week to announce your visit, and it's been amazing, the response. Your event was added late, and we wanted to make sure people knew about it.

Leibovitz: The event was just added on. It was actually Susan that said, "You must go to Portland! You must go to Powell's!" Literally, she said that. I was just visiting three cities or something, but she said I had to go. And it's not a problem because I love Portland.

Dave: We've had so many letters coming in since we announced it. People are worried that they might need tickets. They want to know if you'll sign their books. *Is she really coming? Is she?*

Leibovitz: I just love this book, that it means so many things to so many people. It's very, very moving. It's been a very emotional experience.

I spoke to Annie Leibovitz on the phone a few days prior to her November 23, 1999 appearance at Powell's. I had to be out of town on the day of her visit—a childhood friend was getting married on the other side of the country—so, graciously, Annie agreed to break from a shoot in the middle of an afternoon to call me in Portland. Then, after fans mobbed our Burnside Street store and bought every last copy of *Women* (Annie stayed for hours, talking to every person who'd come), she agreed to sign a hundred more first editions and overnight them from her studio in New York for PowellsBooks.news subscribers. Thank you, thank you, and thank you, again, Annie.

Michael Ondaatje's
Cubist Civil War

◆

Anil's Ghost, Ondaatje's first novel since *The English Patient* captured the 1992 Booker Prize, transports readers to Sri Lanka, dropping us smack in the middle of the island country's brutal civil war. "It is his extraordinary achievement to use magic in order to make the blood of his own country real," Richard Eder wrote of Ondaatje's new novel in *The New York Times Book Review.*

We sat down, and the first thing I said to him was "I have no idea where to start."

Anil's Ghost is a violent, chaotic war story, a page-turning, word-churning flash of a novel. Anil, a forensic anthropologist, "grows up in Sri Lanka," as the author summarized, "goes and gets educated abroad, and through fate or chance gets brought back by the Human Rights Commission to investigate war crimes." The new novel hasn't so much raised the bar on the forensic thriller as moved it to another place entirely.

Thirty years ago, Ondaatje constructed a strange hybrid of a book called *The Collected Works of Billy the Kid* out of snapshots, poems, flyers, interviews, diary entries, and songs. In the three decades since, he's continued bending and stretching the novel into marvelous shapes, building cathedrals of story, mysterious and grand adventures of the everyday. Ondaatje marries poetic instincts with narrative devices like no other novelist writing in English today.

Dave: What was the genesis of *Anil's Ghost*?

Michael Ondaatje: I think it came from the image of someone returning to a country they'd once been a part of, now finding themselves a stranger in that place. That's Anil's path. She grows up in Sri Lanka, goes and gets educated abroad, and through fate or chance gets brought back by the Human Rights Commission to investigate war crimes. That story of the returning stranger seems very central to our time. That was the starting point.

You have someone who is a part of the country and, in a way, has to betray it. It's an odd state to be in, blowing the whistle on your home country. What exactly is the morality? What is your responsibility to the place you come from? Obviously, that is something that concerns me.

I wasn't sure how to write that story, how to write about the war in Sri Lanka. I decided to write from the point of view of people who are not involved in the politics, not involved actively in the war.

Dave: After finishing the novel, I went back and started reading *Handwriting*, your most recent book of poems. There's a lot of common ground between these two books. Obviously, Sri Lanka, but also reoccurring images or ideas. In "Buried," for instance, you use an image that reappears in *Anil's Ghost*, a Buddha statue being unearthed and stolen.

Ondaatje: The books are in some ways a pair, though they seem to be from a different perspective. The poetry, by its nature, is more enigmatic and aphoristic. The novel is much more detailed and tactile, of the present as opposed to the past, forensic in that sense.

But it's a different image in *Handwriting*. One of the metaphors was the burial and stealing of Buddhist statues, how they get stolen and buried, unearthed and resold—like human life, a metaphor for human life. The poems are more archaeological in that way, an archaeological perspective of a war.

Dave: Late in the novel, Gamini talks about how at the end of Western novels and war films the American or Englishman invariably leaves the foreign land and returns home to tell his story. "The war, to all purposes, is over," Gamini says. "That's enough reality for the West."

But *Anil's Ghost* doesn't end there. The narrative continues.

Ondaatje: It's an interesting question: how do you *resolve* a novel? In my early novels, it was easy: Billy the Kid died at twenty-one. That's the end of the novel. Or [in *Coming Through Slaughter*] Buddy Bolden is committed to an asylum.

That's a different kind of resolution than *In the Skin of a Lion* where the book ends with a new starting point, two people driving off into the night and a new life beginning there. In *The English Patient*, there is a new life beginning for Hana and Kip. I don't see novels ending with any real sense of closure. I see the poem or the novel ending with an open door.

I didn't know that Gamini was going to make that speech about American political novels, but, in an odd way, Anil goes off at that point and we just have to stay with the country. It's a responsibility of the writer to get the reader out of the story somehow. It's a balancing act. You don't want to make it too neat or too smug. You want to suggest something new, but at the same time, resolve the drama of the action in the novel.

Dave: What drew me to your novels originally was the way you use structure to tell the stories. It's impossible to predict exactly where they are going next structurally, forward or back, or somewhere off to the side. Often a single line will carry the reader years into the future. How aware are you of the structure as you're writing?

Ondaatje: The structure happens as the story unravels, with each discovery, at each plateau, a sidebar or descant, whatever it is. I did not expect *Anil's Ghost* to go off into a twenty or thirty page section in the Grove of Ascetics when I began, but that seemed to be the way the book should go.

These things are discovered in the actual writing, and they're finessed later on. Once I've discovered the story, I might restructure it, maybe move things around, set up a clue that something is going to happen later, but that happens much later in an editorial capacity. Planning that sort of thing beforehand would bore the hell out of me. If I had it planned beforehand, why would I bother executing it?

It's that kind of odd mix of running with the wave, then later on having the ability to go back and jog it around a bit to make it sharper—to decide when the flashbacks occur, when the scene on the train occurs. I might move a scene like that forward or back a few pages, depending when it seemed right.

Dave: It's a very efficient style. Very suggestive. And it's often nimble enough to allow you to skip over entire scenes. For example, the urinal stones: first Sarath tells Anil about them, then later Palipana mentions them again. When he does, the way you've written it, all of a sudden we're made aware of an entire missing scene. In effect, you've created another whole scene indirectly through a single offhand line of dialogue.

Ondaatje: And that's used as a slight dig at Sarath's interest.

It wasn't planned. I wasn't planning that response, but it seemed…an opportunity. When you're writing, it's as if you're within a kind of closed world. Working on a chapter like the Palipana section, it's just three or four people, but you're getting lots of cross-references and points of view occurring. Sometimes it's the old man's point of view, sometimes it's Anil's, sometimes it's the girl's. The perceptions and ironies double and triple and quadruple. You're getting everyone's point of view at the same time, which, for me, is the perfect state for a novel: a cubist state, the cubist novel.

Dave: Are there other authors you've recognized that in, that you'd feel a kinship with in that sense?

Ondaatje: If you think of a dialogue…In Robert Stone's *Outerbridge Reach* there were moments of wonderful dialogue, or in *Children of Light,* two or three people talking and such wonderful tension in the actual dialogue—you felt a dancing going on. There's a scene of Delillo's, a wonderful fight between a husband and wife that goes on for pages and pages and pages, and you just sense that everything is alive.

It's that kind of state in a novel—you don't try to reach them when you're writing, you can't—but when you see it happening and you're somehow in the middle of the action, that's what you want in some way.

Dave: What do you read? Fiction?

Ondaatje: I read fiction, a little nonfiction, a little poetry—as various as possible. When I was writing this book, the books I *didn't* read were all those forensics books, all those thrillers surrounding us. I began this in 1991 or 1992, and every time I passed a rack of books there seemed to be another forensic thriller. I thought, Oh, Christ! I had to turn away from those.

Dave: Maybe this is what I was trying to get at by talking about structure: when you're writing, working with that blank slate, how much of your energy is channeled toward finding a new way to tell a story? Or is that entirely a product of what the specific story is?

Ondaatje: I think it is a product of the story. *Anil's Ghost* may be a familiar style to earlier books I've written, but it feels new to me. The vocabulary is new. The pacing is different. It feels more muted.

I'm not sure. It has to feel different to me. If I write a scene that seems familiar to something from another book, I'll test it a lot or change it or drop it.

There are situations that are similar to *The English Patient*, certainly, when the characters are all suddenly stuck together. There are moments that are suddenly familiar, but you try to write in a new way, and you try to write something you haven't written before. To take the writing further than you have before.

Dave: In Pico Iyer's new book, *The Global Soul*, he holds *The English Patient* up as a prime example of a new mongrel literature, stories about people who fall into the gaps between cultures. The main characters in that novel exist outside the nationalistic passions of the war; they're physically isolated, too.

In *Anil's Ghost*, there are parallels in Anil's alienation. She doesn't belong in Sri Lanka, and yet, she's as much Sri Lankan as anything else. She has no bearings. Even her name is not her own.

One of the central questions in the book concerns the issue of truth and the perception of it—specifically, public truth versus private truth. It reminded me of what Iyer said in the sense that a person who can detach herself from a nationalist agenda is more independent and perhaps more capable of finding truth.

Palipana talks about truth. Certainly Sarath does. It's a reoccurring issue that seems to underlie the entire story.

Ondaatje: One of the things that happens in novels…it's almost like a continual debate with yourself. That's why you're writing the book. It's why you create characters: so you can argue with yourself.

Where I stand on this issue is somewhere between Sarath and Anil, I suppose. There are various versions of the truth. Gamini's version, also, with his lack of interest in what the truth is or what the politics may be. If someone is dying in front of you, heal them, and if you can't save them then get on to the next one. He's more pragmatic about it. But there's also a historical sense, a kind of moral sense, a political sense— all these versions of the truth.

It's not an abstract discussion. The issue is what these characters, or anyone, will do with the truth. Sarath says, "The truth can be like a flame against a lake of petrol." Truth, at the wrong time, can be dangerous. That's a conflict for Anil, who's used to the more Western sense of holding truth above anything else.

Dave: You mentioned in another interview that you hadn't written poetry for seven years before *Handwriting*. Are you writing now?

Ondaatje: Right now I'm doing nothing. I'm so glad to have crawled out of this book. It took about seven years of pretty intense, tough battling— how to tell the story, what's the right way. It feels like I just finished it. I'm trying to put some distance between that and myself.

Dave: I've been making a list in my head of the scenes or moments in your books that have stayed with me over the years. In *The English Patient*, the description of smelling the underside of a dog's paw: "A bouquet! Great rumours of travel!" I can't tell you how many times I've smelled my dog's feet since I read that.

In *In the Skin of a Lion*, the boy turning on all the lights in his house to attract moths to the screen where he can inspect them up close. I spent a lot of time in the Maine woods growing up, and I would do exactly that. I used to try to explain it to friends. *You watch moths?* When I read the book, I just started recommending it to people instead of trying to make them understand, myself.

I have a very vivid memory of reading "Elimination Dance" in a bathtub and laughing so loud that my roommate asked me through the door what was going on. Readers of *Anil's Ghost* and maybe even *The*

English Patient might be surprised how much fun there is in the poems in *The Cinnamon Peeler*.

Ondaatje: *Anil's Ghost* is a pretty serious book, but you do want to have a break. Even within the book, you have the scenes with Leaf and Anil and their forensic interpretations of movies. It's important to have a break, not just for the reader but for the author as well. Not everything is politics. One has to develop a life.

Dave: When you were younger, writing books like *The Collected Works of Billy the Kid* and *Coming Through Slaughter*, which are almost impossible to categorize or pigeonhole—even your publisher isn't sure exactly what to call *Billy the Kid*; is it a prose poem, a novel, what?—did you have any ideas about what you might want to be writing down the line? Did you have a vision as to how your career might evolve?

Ondaatje: No. When I was writing *Billy the Kid*, all I had was the question, "How do I write this book?" That's always the question. I never think ahead.

Right now, I have no idea what I will write or *if* I will write again. There's a feeling in all the books that everything you know has to go into it. You set everything down, you've done everything, and that's it. It's your last chance. This is the last boat leaving.

Obviously, it has to be somehow connected with the story, but everything you know about passion or politics or love or truth—all those things—somehow must go in that book. So when I finish a novel, whether it's *Anil's Ghost* or *Billy the Kid* or *In the Skin of a Lion*, that's it. I've said everything. I have to start again from scratch. It's a strange state to be in. I'm broke, trying to build again.

Dave: Clearly, you do a lot of research when you're writing a novel—all of them, in one way or another, could be considered Historical Fiction—but always those historical facts are couched within your style; there's a balance of poetics and history. The historical almost becomes poetry.

Ondaatje: It's a very dodgy thing how you do that. I'm not quite sure how it works, if it does, in these books, but it has to be casual. Research can be a big clunker. It's difficult to know how you can make the historical light. Italo Calvino, in his *Memos for the Next Millennium*, has a great essay on lightness. I hadn't read the essay when I was writing this book, but it's an essential principle: you can get bogged down in too much detail.

Even though there's a lot of detail about forensics in this book, it's really just a thin layer. It suggests much more. In fact, you have to keep moving, you have to keep the story going.

Dave: Like swimming.

Ondaatje: Yes, exactly. You trust that this is a good part of the water, but you don't want to sink. You want to get across. There's a great Mickey Spillane quote: "No one ever read a novel to get to the middle."

Dave: How do you feel about the book now that it's finished?

Ondaatje: When you first finish, you have no idea what it's like. Unless you're a flaming egotist, you just don't know. It's difficult to know or judge until several months have passed. That's why the response is important. If everyone hates it, then you probably would start to worry. But it's all you could have done. It's the best you could have written at the time. You hope it will communicate.

Dave: There were many, many of your supporters at McGill when I was in school there, and it was great to discover you so early in your career. I felt like I got in before the rest of the world. Then *The English Patient* suddenly exposed you—all of a sudden, everyone knew who Michael Ondaatje is.

Ondaatje: I'm glad it happened then and not earlier on. I'm not sure how I would have handled the airport recognition scene.

Michael Ondaatje visited Portland on May 23, 2000 to participate in the Portland Arts & Lectures series. In the afternoon, he stopped by the Rare Book Room in our City of Books, then crossed Tenth Avenue to our Internet office and let me pester him for a half-hour about his writing and the arc of his career leading up to the publication of *Anil's Ghost*.

Susan Orlean's
Orchid Adventures

◆

"I'm cynical and skeptical," the author of *The Orchid Thief* explained. "I'm not a joiner. I don't see myself fitting in to some niche."

Susan Orlean is obsessed, just not about orchids. A passionate writer, her unlikely immersion into the South Florida orchid scene produced one of the great regional portraits of recent years, a funny history peopled with land-schemers, drug dealers, heirs to orchid fortunes, international flower hunters (many of whom die on the job), lawyers, legislators, burglars, the only Indian tribe never to surrender to the U.S. government, and a mad genius who aims to clone enough ghost orchids to stock Wal-Mart stores nationwide. Meanwhile, at the center of it all, a murky swamp filled with alligators, poisonous insects, and deadly snakes attracts ravenous collectors who'll risk prison terms to trudge for hours waist deep in standing water, packing orchids into pillowcases and sneaking them out of the state preserve.

"It's about orchids," Orlean admitted, describing her book, "but it's not really about orchids."

Susan Orlean: The Internet didn't exist when I left Portland. I'm beginning to feel like I shouldn't say that anymore because it makes me sound so old.

Dave: When did you leave?

Orlean: 1983. We didn't work on computers at *Willamette Week,* that's for sure. People thought it was a principled stand. *I'm not going to work on computers! That's bad!*

Dave: It's interesting to see readers' comments about your book. The response is generally overwhelmingly positive, but some people get really annoyed that John Laroche disappears from the story for long stretches.

Orlean: It's been funny to read those because I'm curious about what people respond to. To me, it's so clearly the case that this is a subjective telling of this experience. I also think that John Laroche wasn't necessarily the most central character. He does disappear at times.

I'd come across a report of a crime that was so peculiar, that touched so many seemingly incongruous places, communities, and subjects, that writing the book was largely a matter of unpacking those elements. In the process, each element became a story in itself, much more interesting and involved than I would have ever imagined.

I'd casually ask a question, for instance, "What was here before this was the Fakahatchee Strand State Preserve?" imagining that the answer was, "Oh, it was farmland," or, "Oh, it's always just been empty land." Instead, it turned out to be the site of the biggest case of land fraud in American history, filled with its own characters and its own weird poignancy.

The book doesn't follow a linear structure. It follows my curiosity about how this event came to happen. I think a linear book about the subject would have been a complete bore.

Dave: The progression feels natural—or, it did to me. For instance, there's a long digression about the Seminole tribe where you get away from the flowers a bit to tell the story of the chief, but it makes perfect sense to explain more about the Seminoles because they're at the heart of the story.

Orlean: Then to go off from the Seminoles to talk about Chief Billy killing the panther—that law [concerning Native Americans' exemption from certain Florida hunting and collection laws] is what brought Laroche to the Seminoles in the first place and, subsequently, brought them together into the swamp.

I will confess: I like to live a little dangerously as a writer. I don't want to make a digression that I wouldn't think is purposeful—and sometimes it kills you, having information which is so interesting when you know it doesn't organically fit—but this is the way I examined the story. It's very true to the experience I had.

I knew very little about the history of the Seminoles, the laws and the immunity and so forth, and when I started learning about them…Chief Osceola, his persona was so huge. Yes, it was a detour, but it seemed purposeful: what was someone doing collecting Chief Osceola's head? Isn't this again a glimpse back at the idea of orchid collectors in the Victorian era? To me, these parallels built the story.

Dave: How long were you down in Florida?

Orlean: I reported on and off for close to two years. I'd go down for about two weeks at a time, then come back, and while I was back do a lot of the reporting. I tend to do all my reporting before I do my writing.

With this structure, it was more like doing sculpture than drawing. I had to think, If I put this here, I'm not going to have it for there. It was really difficult. I was kind of overwhelmed at first; I thought, I don't know if I can do this.

I wrote out all the information on index cards. I spread them all over. There were certain parts of the book that I absolutely knew would be in there, so I thought, How about if I start off by writing those pieces? That was a dismal failure. I couldn't separate any part of it. I felt like I could only get to the telling of each anecdote if I knew what had come before it and how the reader came to know it.

I almost always write from the beginning to the end. I almost always work the structure out while I'm writing. Maybe that's a risky thing to do, but, for me, the writing is part of learning what I figured out.

Dave: Part of the book's success stems from how informative or educational it is—I don't know what word to use without making it sound dry. That's been a problem when I've tried to explain it to people. I felt like I'd learned a lot; at the same time, it's really entertaining. It's one of the fastest, page-turning books I've read in a long time, which I think is why it works so well—because it's neither one nor the other. It's both.

Orlean: Sometimes I think, Oh God, I don't want people to think they're learning. That's so boring! Why write about it if they could go and look up all the information at the library? Well, because they're not going to. Much the same way you could say, "Why read about the swamp when you could go see it?" Well, most people will never see it. And that's what I do for a living: I go see it and describe it.

Dave: You said writing helps you understand what you figured out. So what did you figure out?

Orlean: That you need to care deeply about something or you're going to feel lost in the universe. I've felt that from my stories before, but this really confirmed it. It's a deep instinct people have: to be able to make sense of this weird, chaotic experience of life, you have to figure out some order, some logic, something to desire. Otherwise, why wake up in the morning?

At the same time, I thought maybe that instinct was disappearing, that people are just too cynical nowadays to feel devoted to something. So maybe it didn't apply anymore. Look at me: I didn't think I was particularly devoted. I love my family and my friends—it's not that I don't care about things—but I don't identify so strongly with any one thing.

I was pleasantly surprised to realize toward the end of this process that that was entirely untrue. Not just a little bit untrue, but so *wildly* untrue that the obviousness of it caught me up short. I'm madly passionate about my work. There's something really important about doing it well, doing it right, and being able to say to someone, "Come read this book. It's about orchids, but it's not really about orchids." That meant so much to me that I was willing to be quite uncomfortable, walking in the swamp, and to be lonely, away from home.

It struck me as almost hilarious to suddenly think, How could I have been so oblivious? Yes, I'm cynical and skeptical. I'm not a joiner. I don't see myself fitting in to some niche. But it was exhilarating to think, Oh, this isn't so strange to me. I get it.

Dave: A reader can see that, but I can understand how you'd completely take it for granted.

Orlean: You forget. It was truly an ingenuous notion on my part.

So what did I figure out? A lot of things, but that was the most personal, the thing that had the most resonance for me. It's corny, but it *is* the process that sustains you. It's not the product.

Dave: You write:

> Many orchid people told me they think CITES [The Convention on International Trade in Endangered Species of Wild Fauna and Flora] is too broad because the real threat to endangered plants is not collectors but rather the loss of wild habitat. Collectors complain that developing countries are plowing down forests as fast as they can, destroying rare plants in the process, and collectors who will retrieve plants out of these areas are the only chance to preserve species that otherwise might vanish forever.

Those collectors blame the inflexibility of laws created by CITES, an organization whose purpose is to help protect the plants, but you don't choose sides in the book. Did you find yourself leaning one way or the other?

Orlean: I didn't want to go into it at great length. For one thing, I didn't feel that I knew enough to be spouting off, but there's no question that making it so complicated and difficult for people to collect plants out of areas being logged out is absurd. Even if people were collecting those plants for profit—and many of these collectors said they'd donate the flowers to botanical gardens—it seems there's an overriding value in not killing things, especially things that may not exist anymore.

There are lots of things about CITES that are important and supportable, but that particular fact was pretty shocking.

Dave: The book presents a very strange, extremely colorful, to be polite, portrait of Florida. Is Florida, especially South Florida, so strange because it's so isolated? That's not a theory you address much in the book.

Orlean: The other day I realized that I'd never explicitly pointed out that it's the only part of the continental United States that's barely attached. Most of it is nowhere near the rest of the United States. There's almost an island mentality there, the sense of being so separate and so surrounded by water. You get the feeling that things can just kind of drift in, or drift out and disappear. There's nowhere on the peninsula that you're not conscious of the ocean.

God knows why it's so weird. It's the heat. It's the way it looks. Nowhere else looks like that in this country, just flat, and the plants are just too big. You go to Alabama and Georgia—they're hot, but they're not tropical. The bottom part of Florida marks the end of the subtropics.

I love the idea that you can create more Florida. Eighty percent of it at one time was actually swamp, and it's just been growing as they fill it in. Someone said to me, "Face it, Florida could break off and float away. It's not inconceivable." It does have that feeling.

Dave: I asked about isolation because I found another book you wrote about a part of the country that's stuck in a corner, and I experienced that place, myself. It wasn't easy to get this, but I grew up in Massachusetts, so I wanted to see it for myself: *Red Sox and Bluefish and Other Things that Make New England New England.*

Orlean: Oh, God. Where did you get that?

Dave: Online, from a book dealer in New Brunswick. As someone who grew up in Framingham—well, you define and contextualize the word *wicked* in here, and it's hard for me not to be appreciative of that kind of documentation.

Orlean: I'd done a column for the [Boston] *Globe,* and it was more or less the day I quit to work on my first book [*Saturday Night*] that Faber & Faber called me and asked about collecting my columns into a book.

It's interesting because someone said to me today, "I was reading some of your early reviews of The Clash when you were at *Willamette Week* in 1978." I sort of cringed and said, "Oh, are they awful?" He said, "No, it sounds just the way you sound now."

Dave: And that was even worse, right?

Orlean: I didn't want to pursue that line of thought. But it's funny to look at this now. Thinking about what is common and what is uncommon, and how ordinary things can also be extraordinary, I guess that's something that's interested me forever.

Someone today was asking if my sister has red hair, and I said that if you don't have red hair you don't realize how much it affects a person. I was half kidding, but it's true that you are different from Day One.

Noticeably different, in a way that people attach personality traits to you. I used to fantasize about having dark hair and brown eyes; that's what I really wanted. When I see little red-haired girls now, I want to say to them, "I understand!"

There might be some common thread about fitting in and not fitting in, belonging and not belonging. Not all nonfiction writers are drawn to these kinds of topics. I don't want to get too psycho-babbly about it, but it's bred in the bone. Someone said, "Oh, you're clever to have done a book like this right when people are so into gardening." Well, the truth is that it was so utterly uncalculated. I just got hooked by the story. What hooks you…it's instinct. It's very organic, and I'm lucky enough to be allowed to write like this.

Dave: How long did you work for *Willamette Week*?

Orlean: I guess it was about three and a half years. I moved to Portland just to take a year off. I'd finished college, and I had nothing to do. I didn't want to go on to graduate school right away. I told my parents I was going to work at a law firm in preparation for law school, which I never had the slightest bit of interest in doing. In the back of my mind, I really wanted to be a writer.

I recently found a notebook I had when I was a senior in college. I'd written,

> What to do after college:
> A. Law school
> B. English graduate school
> C. Writer

With writing, it said, "Pros: Really want to do it. Sounds like fun. Cons: Don't know how to become a writer. Possibility of not earning a living."

Being out here and stumbling on a little magazine that was starting up was incredibly good luck. From there, I started freelancing for some national magazines, then I moved to Boston. I wrote for *The Phoenix*, and I started my first book. Then I moved to New York while I was finishing that one, and I started writing for *The New Yorker* when I was there.

Dave: Okay, we're running out of time, but there are two pages of reading group questions in the back of the paperback edition of *The Orchid Thief*, and I thought it would only be fair to ask you one.

Orlean: Sure.

Dave: Question Number One: Is there a hero in *The Orchid Thief*? An anti-hero?

Orlean: I don't know…How would you describe what a hero is?

Dave: Thirty seconds to answer!

Orlean: Okay. Yes…the hero is finally the ghost orchid for both managing to drag me and half of the human population through horrible swamps to look for it, and at the same time for remaining completely elusive, to this day invisible to me, among others. I'd say that's the hero. And the anti-hero? I don't think there's an anti-hero.

Dave: Good answer.

Orlean: Thanks.

Throughout the course of this conversation, I drank water from an old plastic squirt bottle while Susan sipped from her can of diet cola. Shortly thereafter, Susan read from *The Orchid Thief*, answered questions, and signed books for an appreciative audience in the new Pearl Room at Powell's. All this happened on January 14, 2000.

The World According
to Paul Theroux

◆

Of the fifty travel-related essays, articles, and book reviews in *Fresh Air Fiend*, all but one were written after the publication of Theroux's previous collection, *Sunrise with Seamonsters*, a humbling fact when you consider the range of geographical and thematic coverage within the new book's pages: cross-country skiing through the snowy backwoods of Maine, paddling Pacific islands, following the Zambezi River across Africa, trespassing in Florida, reporting from China before and after Tiananmen Square, then again during the hand-over of Hong Kong.

I'd come across Theroux's critique of William Least Heat-Moon's *PrairyErth* in November, and I was glad for it—it was the most insightful thing I'd found about the book. At the time, that article was one of the only pieces of Theroux's work I'd read other than his famous novel, *The Mosquito Coast*. (His critique of *PrairyErth* is reprinted in *Fresh Air Fiend*.)

Skip forward to May, now, after a couple months of compulsive catching up (Theroux has published more than thirty-five books), thinking about travel and travel writing, and tagging along with the author over hundreds of pages on his adventures around the world. We met shortly before his appearance at Powell's and immediately set out across the neighborhood to a corner store and back, talking about Massachusetts (we both grew up there) and beekeeping (I am not a beekeeper; he is), then settled in for this interview in the Annex.

In conversation as in his writing, Theroux speaks his mind. Having spent nearly forty years roaming the planet, living and traveling amongst whomever would have him, he's earned the right to say he's seen a few things. In fact, he's witnessed first-hand so many of the formative cultural changes of our lifetime. "I thought, I'll never write a blockbuster. I'll never write The Great American Novel," he explained. "What I'd write would reflect where I'd been and what I'd seen—what I know."

Dave: Central to a number of essays in *Fresh Air Fiend* is the idea of becoming a stranger, traveling abroad to escape familiar surroundings, and how that perspective relates to being a writer. When you left Massachusetts in 1963 to enter the Peace Corps, was writing already in your mind as a possible career?

Paul Theroux: Writing was in my mind from the time I was in high school, but more, the idea that I would be a doctor. I really wanted to be a medical doctor, and I had various schemes: one was to be a psychiatrist, another was tropical medicine. I thought tropical medicine would be a way of getting me to another country.

My earliest thought, long before I was in high school, was just to go away, get out of my house, get out of my city. I went to Medford High School, but even in grade school and junior high, I fantasized about leaving. Exploring, camping—I was a Boy Scout with that kind of sleeping-in-a-tent fantasy, which I did. I acted on that. So I had the idea of being a traveler, of going to some exotic place, before I wanted to be a writer. Then the idea of writing began to absorb me.

I saw later, when I became a writer, how being a traveler had helped me. Joining the Peace Corps in sixty-three, going to Africa, that was a very fortuitous thing. Otherwise, I would have been a different person, a different writer. I had wanted to go to Turkey; that was the most exotic place I could think of. Africa was much too far, outside the realm of my thinking, and when I realized I was going, my heart swelled. Just the notion of going. I hadn't thought of it. Central Africa—it was so far away. No tourists went there. People went to Nairobi at that time, to game parks, but not even many of those. I was very lucky to go, and to discover what it meant to write, what it meant to be a stranger.

Dave: When you went to Africa, originally, what was your mission?

Theroux: It was to teach school, to be an English teacher. From sixty-three to sixty-five, I was running a school, basically, in Malawi, in the bush. Later I went to Uganda, where I was an English teacher. I did that for four years. Then I went to Singapore where I was in the English department, again. All the posts were English-related.

But I saw myself as a writer early on. The first things I published were in Africa. In sixty-four, I began to write things for African newspapers and magazines. I sent stories and poetry to the States. In Uganda, I was working on stories and novels. In sixty-six, I submitted my first novel, *Saint Jack*, which was published in sixty-seven. I wrote another novel that appeared in sixty-eight, and another appeared in sixty-nine. When I went to Singapore, I was still writing about Africa. It was a continuous process.

I thought, I'll never write a blockbuster. I'll never write The Great American Novel. What I'd write would reflect where I'd been and what I'd seen—what I know. But I didn't write about myself. My early main characters were not like me. There was an Indian, a Chinese, a French-Canadian revolutionary, an insurance man, a pimp in Singapore...

Dave: You found, eventually, a kind of literary community in Africa. You mention in the book a number of writers you met while you were there. Was that because of the relative isolation, do you think? Because you were so far away?

Theroux: That's an interesting question because I never thought of it as a literary community. I thought of it as people who were also writing and who were friends of mine. I read what they wrote, and they read what I wrote. It's interesting how distinguished they were to become. Nadine Gordimer got the Nobel Prize. Wole Soyinka got the Nobel Prize. She was in South Africa; he was in Nigeria. Another man, Rajat Neogy, ran a magazine there and became a very distinguished editor. It's really amazing.

They seemed, at the time, very good writers, of course, but…in Uganda, very few writers came through there. It wasn't literary society. There were maybe half a dozen writers. The most significant one was V.S. Naipaul. I met him in sixty-six. That was a very big deal for me, meeting him.

But there weren't a lot of writers. One of the virtues of the place was that there were just a few, and most of the people didn't read, didn't write, didn't care about it. Writing meant nothing. That was a virtue because I was left on my own. It wasn't like living in New York or Paris or London where everyone was writing and you'd have the sense of competition. I just felt: I'm in this interesting place, wild things are happening. It was the sixties; it was intense, politically. Tremendous good fortune, really.

Dave: Since then, you've been all over the world. Just in this book, if you were to mark the places you've been with pins on a map, you'd cover a good part of the globe.

Theroux: There'd be a lot of pins.

Dave: And you're still traveling. How have these trips evolved for you? How far ahead do you plan? Do you find yourself in one place, yearning to visit another?

Theroux: Like that, yes. Thinking about it, dreaming about it. There are places that I've always wanted to go. First I went to Africa, and when I was there I realized there were places in Africa I really to wanted to visit: The Congo, West Africa, Mombassa. I wanted to see the deep, dark, outlandish places. In the early seventies, I wanted to go to India. I thought, Imagine, just going up and down India on a train. Fantastic! Ditto the Soviet Union and China.

I don't have a job. I've been able to act on impulse. And my wife was very helpful, my first wife. We had little kids, and she didn't say, "Don't go." She said, "That's your job. Do it."

This book, *Fresh Air Fiend*, covers fifteen years. A previous book, *Sunrise with Seamonsters*, covers twenty years. That's thirty-five years of traveling. It's true, there'd be a lot of pins in the map, but that's a lot of years, thirty-five years. For all that time, I've gone to maybe half a dozen places a year. Six times thirty-five. And many years I did more than that. I never did less.

I've never spent a whole year in one place without leaving. Even when I was in Singapore, where I worked for three years, I went to Borneo, I went to Indonesia and Bali, I went to Sumatra, I went to Thailand, I went to Burma. I went all over Malaysia. I traveled throughout Southeast Asia while I was living in Singapore. Took a train to Bangkok, flew to Rangoon. I had no telephone, no secretary. I was just teaching, and if I had time off I went somewhere.

How did it happen? I'm a compulsive traveler—not terribly well-organized, but I was alone. I didn't care where I slept. I felt I could handle it. I didn't need a big organization; I wasn't signing up for trips. I heard there was a boat going to Kota Kinabalu—*KK*, they call it in Borneo. I said to my wife, "There's a boat that goes every two weeks and I'd like to get it." She said, "Okay."

Then I decided to somehow make it pay. I remember when I went to Burma the first time, probably about 1968, I thought, I should really write something. So I wrote something for *The Atlantic Monthly*. I think I got three hundred dollars, which probably didn't even pay for the plane, but I was defraying my expenses. I wasn't making a living.

Anyone can do it, travel, but you have to resign yourself to the fact that you're not going to be networking. You'll probably never get rich. To rise in the world, you have to stay in a city. Monica Lewinsky's career is an interesting example. She networked with someone who was a fundraiser. She got a job at The White House. Then she got transferred to The Pentagon. Then she got a job at Revlon. Granted, she had a little help along the way, but she was twenty-two years old. When I was twenty-two, I was teaching in a school in Africa with no prospects whatsoever.

If you want to hang in there and "make it"—and I'm not talking about doctors and lawyers because you need education for that—you stick around powerful people and they move you along. They help. That's how it happens. You make the right friends. It's kissing a lot of butt, swapping business cards, playing golf. I've never done it. My kids haven't done it. I'd be very depressed if they did.

Dave: And yet you have met a lot of writers along the way.

Theroux: I have, but the more writers you meet, the more you think that writers are cranks, weirdos, no-hopers waiting to get invited out to dinner. As a group, writers are not big, powerful people. They look it, perhaps, because of their books, but who are they? *I* have great regard for them, but the average person doesn't give a shit one way or the other.

Dave: One of the really funny things in the book—you talk a lot about the general nature of writers, and you mention some of the words critics have used to describe you in various reviews: cantankerous, grouchy, sour and impatient, irritating and impolite. Reading through this collection, I don't really take that from your writing.

Theroux: I'm glad. People are constantly saying it, but I think American reviewers are lazy. Many of them, I think, don't even read the whole book.

For example, I have a reputation for being sarcastic. Well, I don't think I am. I think *ironic* would be a better word. Ironic is a veiled kind of sarcasm, and it has a lot of humor in it. But we, as an American nation, aren't known for our irony. It looks cruder than it is, and it's a problem for some people.

Dave: I was recently in New Zealand, though, reading this book, and the reaction I always got was, "Oh, Theroux, he's the one who wrote such awful things about Kiwis."

Theroux: What happened in New Zealand…I wrote about their Governor General. I had dinner with her, and she spent the whole time bad-mouthing John Kennedy. She said, "I'm reading this book about him. He was a womanizer!"

I said, "Well, I'm as interested as anyone in that kind of thing, but that's not Kennedy's whole career. He did many things. He was a leader, he was in the war. Just to say that he was a womanizer is really not saying very much. It's not the whole truth."

She said, "Well, I definitely believe that this should be published."

So I asked her, "What if it was you? What if people wrote about your personal life that way?"

She said, "I'm a politician. Let them write."

Well, we were eating all the while, and she was picking her teeth, belching. I described her saying this and the way she looked, the way she was acting at the table, all the things she was saying. She didn't know I was a writer. Kiwis didn't like it; they thought it was a low blow. I thought it was pretty funny, actually.

Dave: A reoccurring theme in *Fresh Air Fiend* concerns the idea of telling the truth—and I'm not referring to anything you may have written about New Zealand or any particular person, but about travel writing, in general. Ultimately, you found that you have to write truthfully about what you witness as a traveler. That's the final criterion.

Theroux: You write what you see, even though it may seem absurd or may contradict received wisdom.

For example, people write about England, and they may say, "He's so British. He's so polite." Actually, the British can be very polite, but they can also be very rude. Life can be extremely peaceful there; it can also be pretty rough on a Saturday afternoon if you wind up on a train with a bunch of football hooligans banging on the windows, breaking bottles, and puking on your shoes. That's not very "English." You can have any kind of experience in England, from the most refined to the most barbaric. But a lot of people don't want to see the other side.

When I lived there, I was always looking for Dickensian London, or refinement. What I found was the English, who are not one thing but many. That's more interesting to me. You write about it from the inside, and you tell the truth. A lot of people might not like it, but it's not my job to please them.

Dave: "Chinese Miracles," the essay in *Fresh Air Fiend*—to me that was the high point of the book. There was so much in there, the writing evoked those rising cities and the state of China's economic boom more tangibly than anything I've read about the subject. We're always reading in the news about American manufacturers operating plants in China, cheap labor in China, but your essay put a human face on it, contextualized it, and made it real in a way that others don't. I felt like I could see those cities rising, the half-finished scaffolding and dust blowing in the wind.

Theroux: I'm glad to hear you say that. I hope that it helps people to understand where China was when I wrote it, which was in ninety-two.

Dave: Have you been back since then?

Theroux: Not to manufacturing China, no. I was in Hong Kong when it got handed over—and I wrote about that experience in "Ghost Stories," the essay that follows "Chinese Miracles."

I haven't been back to the Special Economic Zones, but those places are all established, and there are more of them now. China is an incredibly dynamic place, but you can also see it's an ecological monstrosity. You can't put up cities and have that much manufacturing without completely destroying the agricultural base—or cutting down a lot of trees, having floods, dislocating a lot of people, having pollution. Animals die, people get sick. It completely destroys the fabric of a country when you have unlimited growth, but it's amazing in that this is what everyone wants to happen. This is development.

Dave: The collection closes with a series of essays about some of the major travel books of our time and the writers who have influenced you—Bruce Chatwin, Graham Greene, and V.S. Pritchett, to name a few. Who's doing this kind of thing now that interests you? You mention in the book that you don't read much travel writing.

Theroux: I don't read much travel writing particularly because I don't want to read interpretations of places that I want to go. I don't want someone to mediate and interpret the place for me before I see it. But I read Jonathan Raban—he's a friend of mine, and I like his work. Jan Morris is interesting. Mostly, I tend to read older books and guide books, *Lonely Planet* guides and things like that.

The thing I do most is look at maps. I study them. If I'm going to a place, I get all the maps and look at them. There's a lot of information on a map.

Paul Theroux visited Powell's City of Books on May 18, 2000. Before
sitting to talk about *Fresh Air Fiend*, we walked together to Georgia's
Grocery at SW Stark Street and 12th Avenue to pick up a can of
Tecate. The author was thirsty; he wanted a little beer. Who was I
to stop him?

Learn More

———————— ◆ ————————

Powell's Books, an independent bookseller since 1971, stocks more than a million used, new, and out-of-print titles at its Portland, Oregon locations for sale locally and online. Powells.com features hand-picked, recommended titles at up to 70% off, as well as hundreds of staff picks and regular contests. (Prizes range from round trip airfare and luxury accommodations in downtown Portland to autographed first editions of acclaimed new releases and credit to spend at Powells.com.) You'll also find more installments of the exclusive author interview series represented in this volume. And Powells.com offers free worldwide shipping on orders of $50 or more.

Yahoo! Internet Life magazine recently called Powells.com **the best source for used books on the Web.** We add thousands of affordable, top-quality, used titles to the shelves every day. Find new and used editions side by side or browse our entire inventory of used volumes within your favorite store sections. Browse among only those used books acquired in the last two weeks and find the best deals first.

Powell's Rare Book Room offers thousands of autographed editions, out-of-print classics, and other hard to find gems, many dating back to past centuries. *Time* magazine called Powells.com "**a must for out-of-print editions.**"

Each week, we restock the shelves of our Bestseller room with our readers' twenty favorites. What are people reading? At Powells.com, the answer tends to include some surprises. You'll also find further recommendations from our staff: great, lesser-known titles you might like to read after enjoying the bestsellers.

Special, web-only features include immediate download of electronic books and a wide array of **timely content** from our section hosts, notable international publications including *Utne Reader, Mother Jones, Poets & Writers, Escape* magazine, *New Dimensions Public Radio, 24framespersecond, The Black World Today, Sportsjones,*

BlueEar.com, the *A & E Book Club*, Douglas Brown's *Factoids from the Natural World*, and Djangos.com.

Your privacy and security is guaranteed at Powells.com. The personal information you submit to our web site will not be shared, sold, or disclosed to third parties in any form, for any purposes, at any time. Powell's will not disclose your sales history or email address to third parties for any purposes, at any time. Records of the items you purchase will not be shared with other businesses or customers, period, online or off.

Powell's has built its outstanding reputation on almost thirty years of personal service. Powells.com's secure server, certified by Verisign®, provides the highest level of security available. We guarantee that every transaction you make at Powells.com will be 100% safe.

Anchored on Portland, Oregon's West Burnside Street, Powell's City of Books is the largest used and new bookstore in the world—a very fun place to spend the day, whether it's raining or not.

Literacy Volunteers of America (LVA), Inc. is a national network of local volunteer literacy programs that assist adults and their families to acquire literacy skills through professionally trained and managed volunteer tutors. LVA is committed to:

- increasing literacy for adults and their families;
- effectively utilizing and supporting volunteers in the delivery of services;
- providing research, training, and technical assistance related to the various aspects of literacy.

By accomplishing this mission, LVA enables students to achieve personal, educational, and job-related goals.

The majority of the adult learners served by LVA receive basic literacy instruction. LVA's target population is made up of adults who read at Level One, the lowest of five levels described by the U.S. Department of Education in the National Adult Literacy Survey of 1993. According to that survey, over forty million adults in this country, or twenty-one to twenty-three percent, are at Level One. They cannot read basic signs or maps, complete simple forms, or carry out many of the tasks required of an adult in our society.

LVA offers a professionally designed and field-tested workshop that enables volunteers to tutor basic literacy students. After being matched with an adult learner, tutors receive regular support and additional opportunities for training through the local LVA affiliate. In thirty-eight years of providing free, individualized tutoring services, LVA has proven that professionally trained and supported volunteers can be effective tutors. More than half a million lives have been changed as a result.

Learn more about LVA...
on the web at www.literacyvolunteers.org

by phone: (315) 472-0001
toll-free: (877) HELP-LVA

or write to:
Literacy Volunteers of America
635 James Street
Syracuse, NY 13203-2214

Book Sense™ is an effort uniting independent bookstores across the country to raise awareness of the unique qualities that have always set us apart from corporate chains: knowledge, passion, community, personality, and character.

Independent booksellers bring years of knowledge about books to their jobs and can provide expert advice on your selections. *The Book Sense 76*, a diverse and provocative selection of books personally recommended by independent booksellers across the country, is just one great resource. Check out our Staff Picks pages at Powells.com to find hundreds of booksellers' favorites, old and new.

Independents are recognized for their passionate recommendations of the books they love. Any independent bookseller will tell you that their joy comes from turning someone on to a new author or a great new literary gem. We stake our integrity on these selections.

An independent bookstore is also an invaluable asset to its community. A healthy independent bookstore doubles as a vital community resource: as a gathering place for family and friends, as a supporter of local causes and associations, and as a center for community activities like readings and special events. Here's just one example: every November, when you say "It's for Kids!" at checkout, Powell's donates ten percent of the sale price to local school library funds. Thanks to this annual program, our public school library budgets have increased more than seventy-five percent!

No one independent bookstore is like any other—this, too, offers reason for celebration. Independent bookstores each have their own personality and character; each inspires a feeling of serendipity and surprise. Why? Because they're built by readers, for readers. Imagine the luxury—building your dream bookstore, showcasing the books you

think others would want to read. We're thrilled—and honored—to take
on that responsibility.

Visit Book Sense™ online at **www.booksense.com** to find the independent bookstore nearest you.

Pantheon Books: *Waiting* by Ha Jin ©1999 by Ha Jin. *A Clever Baseballist: The Life and Times of John Montgomery Ward* by Bryan Di Salvatore ©1999 by Bryan Di Salvatore.

PublicAffairs: Line from *A Cure for Gravity* by Joe Jackson ©1999 by Joe Jackson. Reprinted by permission.

Random House: Excerpt from *The Orchid Thief* by Susan Orlean ©1998 by Susan Orlean. Reprinted by permission. *Midnight in the Garden of Good and Evil* by John Berendt ©1994 by John Berendt. *The Everlasting Story of Nory* by Nicholson Baker ©1998 by Nicholson Baker. *Women* by Annie Leibovitz and Susan Sontag, photographs ©1999 by Annie Leibovitz, text ©1999 by Susan Sontag.

Rob Weisbach Books: *Music for Torching* by A.M. Homes ©1999 by A.M. Homes

Simon & Schuster: Excerpts from *Squandering Aimlessly: My Adventures in the American Marketplace* by David Brancaccio ©2000 by David Brancaccio. Reprinted by permission. *We'll Meet Again* by Mary Higgins Clark ©1999 by Mary Higgins Clark.

Viking Penguin: *Bridget Jones's Diary* by Helen Fielding ©1996 by Helen Fielding. *A Star Called Henry* by Roddy Doyle ©1999 by Roddy Doyle.

Excerpt from "Why We Travel" by Pico Iyer ©1998 by Pico Iyer. First published in *The Los Angeles Times Magazine*, April 19, 1998. Reprinted by permission.